What others are saying about KARMA Covered Candy:

"Delightful and expansive, KARMA Covered Candy is a delicious treat for all serious seekers of truth."
> Carolyn Anderson, Executive Director
> Global Family

"Unparalleled journey through the pitfalls of love, Richard Treadgold lays down his life so that others may laugh and learn."
> Gloria St. John
> Author of <u>The Path of Parenting</u>

"A must read for everyone with 'pictures' of the perfect love. . . . Especially valuable for such men, and the women who love them."
> *Charlotte Tyler*
> *Attorney, Environmental Law*

"Delightful, intriguing, easy to ready and. . . hard to put down. . . . Full of heart and spirit (as well as mind.)"
> Ellen Clephane, Ph.D. (Candidate)
> Family and Relationships Therapist

". . . .(this) work is admirable. KARMA Covered Candy is witty, charming, thoughtful, and ever so personal."
> Charles Odenthal, Psy.D.
> Clinical Psychologist

"When I wasn't laughing, I was underlining. A wonderful contribution. . . . Thank you."
> Rhonda Mikalaitis, Co-Founder
> Earth and Sky Wilderness Trips

ALSO BY RICHARD TREADGOLD

Connecting At The Heart
(A Core Group Manual)

TOTAL EMPOWERMENT:
A Complete Guide to Success, Love & Happiness*

*To be published later this year. See back pages of book.

KARMA
Covered
Candy

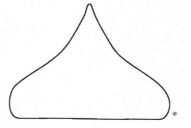

KARMA
Covered Candy

(Conquering An Addictive Love)

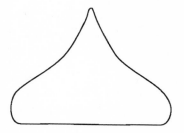

by
Richard Treadgold

Essence Foundation
San Francisco, CA USA

Self-Empowerment Training
For seminar information write to Essence Foundation.
(See back pages of book.)

Published by Essence Foundation
P. O. Box 16418
San Francisco, CA 94116.   4/96

Cover Design - Author
Cover Graphics Production - Abacus, Inc.
Printing - Griffin Printing & Lithograph Co., Inc.

Library of Congress Cataloging in Publication Data
LC Catalog Card Number 91-07017C
        Treadgold, Richard
            KARMA Covered Candy
            (Conquering An Addictive Love)

    ISBN 1-879647-77-X

This edition is printed on acid-free paper that meets the American
National Standards Institute 239.48 Standard.

> Essence Foundation and the author, in association with
> various environmental agencies, will facilitate the planting of
> a tree for every tree used in the manufacturing of this book.

To Marion
My Beloved Life-Partner In Unconditional Love

As we soar our separate skies
On tempered wings from tethered tries
One thing remains forever true
Within my heart I dream of you

and

To Tayne
My Brother Argonaut

Contents

That sweet seduction is what we feel,
When seeking a love to prevent life's hurt,
And we gobble it down as if our last meal,
With Karma Covered Candy our just desert.

Introduction

Woven into my earliest memories is the annual, large box of assorted chocolates that would inevitably show up during the Christmas holidays. Nuts and chews were my favorites; but, since they were always mixed in with creams and other gooey impostors mimicking real candy, I would have to carefully guess where those good ones were hiding. I got so that I could tell a few by their shape, however the only sure way of course was to bite into them. And no amount of chocolate coating could compensate for the disappointment of guessing wrong and suddenly having a mouthful of that unwanted, overly-sweetened ooze. When this happened, I would become uncommonly quiet and, with a Cheshire expression, head for the nearest unoccupied bathroom, there to deposit the counterfeit concoction down some unsuspecting drain.

Many of us approach life the same way—easily seduced by those irresistible ingredients within the assorted circumstances of life, like love for instance, which will (when correctly chosen of course) provide the special flavor of happiness that fate has prepared just for us. However, the good selections are invariably mixed in with others that aren't so palatable. Often, after that first good bite we are seized with the impulse to take the sticky, unsavory result of our choice and flush it from our lives at the earliest opportunity. And, although this bitter-sweet process is painful, we seem unable to resist its alluring promise and, with even greater hunger, quickly select another. ·

This book is a short chronicle of the journey to discover what life is really all about. If you are one who also seeks to truly feast on the love and destiny meant for you and are tired of merely nibbling addictively on the abundant, sugar-filled confections that enticingly crowd the prescribed paths in life, then you may discover some surprises hidden in these pages that will guide you in experiencing the truths about the candy you are drawn to select, and that one, truly remarkable relationship awaiting your embrace.

•   •   •

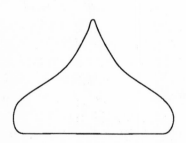

Life promises nothing, yet offers so much,
Just one of its many riddles, my friend,
Like a circle, a cycle, a spiral and such,
Its beginning is found when we reach the end.

Chapter One

The End of Circles

Statistically, I had been living the "American dream" for quite some time, having been married three times, switched jobs seven times, finagled two graduate degrees, loved chocolate in any form, owned four homes in succession, took two vacations a year, slept an average of 7.2 hours a night, consumed a six-pack now and then, spent more than I earned, always seemed to have a dog or cat as a good friend, continually battled with calories, and spent at least fifteen minutes each month contemplating the relevance of God. How, one might ask, could such a life be so terrible that it called for the drastic step of suicide?

I suppose it wasn't a total surprise to me, as I sat in the Denver airport that cold March morning, trying to decide the most expedient, but painless, method of accomplishing this dramatic exit. Like Charlie Brown in the Peanuts comic strip when the pop-fly ball is heading in his direction and he's saying to himself, "I know I'm going to drop it, I know I'm going to drop it. . . ." And, of course, his greatest fear comes true. I had always thought that my greatest fear was not being able to find the woman of my dreams. However, when she finally did come into my life, amazingly I realized I had an even greater apprehension—that of losing the woman of my dreams. So, there I was, like good ole Charlie after he's muffed the catch, feeling alone in the comical valley of despair, lost in anger and disbelief, yet somehow having known all along that what I so terribly dreaded would come true.

Probably from birth I knew there was something I was here to do, some mark I was to make on the world; but how was I to find it and how fulfilling could it be without that special person with whom to share it? I guess in a way I thought of this person as my soulmate, although I would have been hard pressed to define that term. I only knew that now, after searching all my life for her (though it felt even longer) and before I could actually embrace my divine, still unknown fate, I was losing the one beautiful and necessary key I felt I needed to unlock my destiny. I couldn't imagine another special person divinely designated just for me; and, on the off chance that there was and I did happen to find her, what guarantee was there that I wouldn't lose her, too? Yes, in that one, interminable dark moment, permanently escaping the human dilemma seemed eminently logical.

To the other preoccupied travellers in the busy terminal, however, I admit my drastic intentions might have been deemed a bit over-reactive. Most people, I'm sure, would have unhesitatingly traded lives with me, seeing my present circumstance, as painful as it was, more filled with opportunities than obstacles. I had saved enough money to live (moderately) without the necessity of an eight to five job for maybe a couple of years. I was in my early forties, enjoyed fantastic health, and was also exceptionally good looking, with just a very slight tendency toward self-deception.

Dejected, I looked down at the thick, brightly colored ticket envelope, absent-mindedly using it to tap a nervous rhythm on the dull black armrest attached to an otherwise empty row of molded plastic chairs. The protruding pale green boarding pass had the usual computer printing where almost every word is some type of code or abbreviation, making it very difficult to understand except for a large, bold "NON-REFUNDABLE" diagonally stamped across the top.

Since it was obvious that these vouchers, even if unused, could not add to the value of my estate, the only sensible course of action was to postpone the execution of my more final departure until I got to Boston, and then only after going to at least one of its great sea food restaurants. (No one deserves to have their last meal catered by Continental Airlines.)

My decision to make this trip had been made several months earlier. Then, the idea of attending a seminar entitled "Becoming Empowered" seemed logical; but, as one might expect from such a theme, it now held the ominous prospect of creating fissures in my current determination to self-destruct. However, once landed at Logan Airport and alert to the prospect of its potential insidious influence, I resolved to attend the scheduled two-and-a-half-day event as my last positive action in this world. I could participate free from all notions that life was fair and just, and that happiness could be sustained, and that love could be trusted. I had seen the basic fabric of my tattered life and found it to be merely tangled threads of chaos and illusion. I would be at this gathering as one with nothing to lose, because I knew there was nothing to gain. It was a tremendous relief not to be a victim of life anymore; I could finally stop chasing those fairytale promises about relationships, which, like large, illusive carrots, had always remained just beyond my grasp. I walked in actually feeling sorry for the lovely, well-meaning (but unsuspecting) seminar leaders, who were going to try to teach me anything.

But, despite being in the midst of twenty strangers and in my thickest cloud of despair, I inexplicably found myself joyful, spontaneous, witty, and energetic. In short, I felt truly alive. "This is the way to go out," I started telling myself. I even began deriving some perverse pleasure knowing how everyone at the seminar was going to be surprised at how someone so "together" could do something like "that." Unfortunately, or I guess I should say fortunately, life played another of its tricks on me—one of those little, sneaky numbers that we know it's doing, but we're so intrigued that we can't prevent it. There was this woman at the seminar. . . .

She was a lawyer (Harvard, no less), a professional singer, an actress, and an astrologer. She was pretty, vivacious, intelligent, seductive, and also wealthy (though I had to take her word for this last attribute.) But, it was one of her other virtues that proved to be my Waterloo—she was instantly attracted to me. I'm not sure exactly when, but sometime during that first day of the workshop the thought occurred to me, "Maybe it would be best if I postponed my planned demise until I got back to Denver."

I stayed in Boston for an extra day or two, and we spent the entire time in bed; although sex really didn't play much of a part in what we shared. We snuggled and laughed and talked endlessly. I was fascinated by how quickly we became intimate. We shared each moment fully in a way that I thought was possible only with a soulmate. I knew I was savoring each drop of time, partly because I anticipated my impending finale, but something more was happening; she was just part of it. I had actually enjoyed and connected in a deep way with almost everyone in the seminar, much more so than I would have normally. It was very surprising and equally disturbing to me that in letting go of my desire live I had apparently become more lovable, and more loving. . . .

•   •   •

The plane ride back to Denver was restless and confusing. I had committed to go through with this morbid plan and, therefore, was experiencing some pressure to proceed as a matter of principle. I was, if nothing else, someone who kept his word. Certainly some of the uneasiness I felt was just the customary anxiety of what lay beyond the threshold of death, but that wasn't it. Even though I had accepted being defeated by life, I just couldn't believe the contest had been so one-sided. Obviously I had missed some important road signs along the way and wandered off the designated course to my appointment with destiny, which I pictured still waiting like an anxious bride, hidden behind vague Karmic veils at the elusive altar of happiness.

I extended the seat back the full six inches and, through the scratched plexiglass window, watched the typical urban scenery until the altitude made everything on the ground monotonous. There were a few dog-eared magazines protruding from the elastic pouch on the seat in front of me that the compulsive passenger to my right quickly retrieved with my passive blessing. Within a few minutes the movie, *Moonstruck*, was showing. I decided to try to sleep, although I knew it would be a waste of time. . . . Being restless, I soon opened my eyes to see Cher receiving a rose from her smiling boss. I didn't have a headset on but I knew roughly what was being said from having seen the movie twice before. However, as I watched this time, there seemed to be so much more going on behind the dialogue. All the characters seemed to have so many feelings and thoughts remaining unsaid in their expressions, yet wanting to be heard; and I suddenly felt the familiar, seductive presence of hope.

"That's it," I finally realized. If I could look at my life as if it were a movie, reviewing it carefully enough, honestly enough, I could discover the overlooked truths hidden in the shadows or whispered between the lines that could explain my current calamity. Without the truth, I could see that my life would remain just a series of circles. But, if I had the truth, maybe I could do something about it. I had to know. So with the determination that comes from the belief that nothing is at risk, I sat back, closed my eyes, and began scanning through the stored archives of my heart and mind. . . .

I was raised by my mother and her parents in a religiously (Christian) inclined household. Well actually, describing them as religiously inclined would be the same as referring to the Pacific Ocean as a pond. Fortunately for me, my older brother received the bulk of their eager spiritual guidance.

I had two great preoccupations while growing up—sex and nature. Well, to be more precise, I had but one of those obsessions, and only when wanting a respite from those confusing and demanding sexual rituals would I venture out into nature. Even with all my fantasizing, the whole area of sex remained mostly a forbidden fog in which to cautiously explore when no one was looking. It was one sleepy night at age fifteen when I discovered the fabled male orgasm (quite accidently I should add in deference to any living relatives) by rolling over in bed and inadvertently squeezing my penis between my legs in such a way that, after about ten minutes or so, it exploded in a frighteningly pleasurable way. The first time it happened I wondered quite seriously if I had done some real damage, but somehow had the presence of mind not to call out for help. Although this sleep-inducing ritual was replicated with adolescent exuberance many times in the months that followed, it would be quite some time before I would enjoy this peril without being alone.

That magical and irreversible step through the carnal entrance to adulthood occurred at age seventeen. She was a neighborhood girl, younger than I but "old for her age" as they say. Seeing her bright, engaging smile as I watched this movie of my past, I now wanted to say so many things to her; although I couldn't remember us ever talking very much at the time. We both wanted more love in our lives, and physical affection seemed an appropriate alternative. I do remember our time alone as a sanctuary from my compulsive teenage duties. A respite where I could melt into her blossoming femininity, fleeting though those moments were because of my emerging need to be a man, which insisted that I control this beautiful girl. When angry, I subscribed to the standard male procedure of acting wounded and giving her the silent treatment; but, because of hormonal intervention, this tactic was usually employed only until the weekend.

We never used condoms, probably because I was too self-conscious to buy them. Besides, I just knew that fumbling around with a "rubber" would deflate the mood. Ignoring her polite concerns, I proposed instead that I could control my orgasm and withdraw prior to the point of no return, thereby eliminating the need for such primitive precautions. (After all, I did have at least two good years of practice.) Although my resolve in the matter was commendable, this noble plan would frequently be abandoned at the very moment it was most needed. Afterward, in panic and forced to rely on my limited knowledge of chemistry, I would rush to the drugstore and with no embarrassment at all purchase a small bottle of Lavoris mouthwash. Then, I would cajole my beloved to make use of this red, acidic liquid in a way probably not envisioned by the manufacturer and certainly not described on the label. Because she never got pregnant, there is a likelihood that Lavoris could be sold as a spermicide; but, judging from her formidable resistance to this almost weekly procedure, I'm sure it would be one hell of a marketing challenge for Madison Avenue.

Looking back I felt sad to know that this special person with whom I shared such a magical and important time in life never heard me say how grateful I was for those brief moments of closeness, and for the many aspects of myself that were awakened through our intimacy. One of the most compelling of these was a dream, actually more like a vision, which began to appear around this time in my life, and at regular intervals ever since.

It starts with a distant alluring melody, unmistakable and haunting. The strange music seems to form into a floating, violet sphere that slowly descends into view. Becoming visible within the opaque bubble is a tall, willowy figure of a woman with dark, loosely flowing silken robes. She is barefoot, joyfully dancing in a rhythmic motion as her eyes sparkle behind an angelic face lost in the soft compelling music. She smiles at me lovingly and invitingly, but without any impatience. Her dance continues, and within the sphere several brilliant rainbows appear, slowly rotating to overlap like velvet petals, each seemingly holding the promise of everything I could ever want. I knew then, and was reminded every time it reappeared, that this dream meant that there was a special person for me, and that my destiny lay just beyond.

"Typical American childhood," I assured myself while smiling apologetically to the stewardess for not having pulled down my window shade for the convenience of the movie viewers. Doing so, I took another quick glance at Cher, who was resigning to her fate of marriage and saying a temporary farewell to her fiancé at the airport. I then shut my eyes to return to my own screen. With the credits of my early years over, an intriguing opening scene immediately grabbed my attention. It was one of those "forks in the road" where we have to make an important choice and then often return to second-guess ourselves. . . .

•   •   •

When I reached the scary age of eighteen, my mother, free now in her own mind to remarry and move away, did just that; although she left in her place a typical unseen maternal pressure within me to "do the right thing." This meant getting married and, as quickly as possible, making her a grand-mother. It also meant becoming a priesthood member in her church. Now, I did know I was alive to do something important with my life but, although I had absolutely no clue as to what that might be, I remained unconvinced of my mother's scenario. Marriage and children were too common-place and, more importantly, church life appeared exceed-ingly mundane, not that her church was different than any other organized religion, for essentially it wasn't. However, to be fair to God, I decided that if He wanted me to head in a particular spiritual direction I would give Him ample opportunity to make that clear.

I wouldn't say that at this point in my life I had a great connection with God; it was mostly an unspoken bond through my many communal excursions into nature. I did pray once in a while, usually just before school exams for which I hadn't studied; but, judging from my grade-point average (C-), I knew that at best He only heard my prayers a little less than half the time. However, for the importance of the occasion, I returned to the woods and again attempted contact. This was the first time that I remember earnestly wanting God to reveal Himself, to talk to me directly so that I would know I was on the right course.

After half an hour of uneventful observation, I felt deserted. I began praying for any sign just to let me know that He existed. When nothing happened, I took it as an indication that the path to my special destiny was simply to do whatever I felt like doing; and, failing to see the self-serving nature of such an assumption, I marched from the forest, probably amidst falling trees and striking lightning. Within a month I had taken the responsible steps of getting a full-time job, enrolling in college, and buying a brand new, red Plymouth convertible—on credit. Unfortunately, within a few more months I was on academic probation at school and my car was consuming more money than I made. Something needed to change.

I knew from his infrequent contact over the years that my dad, long ago divorced from my mother, lived in Southern California where he enjoyed what I fantasized to be the affluent life-style of a bank executive. Obviously, the time had come to renew old acquaintances.

He was at first very glad to see me and, as one might predict, invited me to come and live with him while continuing my education. However, it wasn't long before events began to strain our unfamiliar father-son relationship. When my transcripts arrived and he discovered my grades were somewhat less than the A- average he anticipated (evidently misperception partly created by his not yet being familiar with my endearing tendency to embellish the truth) he became surprisingly surly and insisted I take a diagnostic battery of tests at UCLA, ostensibly to reveal the most appropriate educational direction for my particular intelligence quotient. However, it seemed to me, as with any business venture, that he really wanted to find out the odds of his investment ever paying off. The prognosis of this three-day psychological inspection concluded that I probably could make it through college, so he cautiously agreed to assist me in this endeavor. He had, of course, an idea of the son he wanted; and, likewise, I knew what a father should be like. After about a year of trying to match those pictures, we both knew we were equally disappointed.

Once back in San Francisco, Vietnam consumed the next big chunk of my life, three years to be exact, although I never got closer to it than the TV set. I spent that time fighting the draft and passively protesting the war. My family wanted me to enlist as part of my patriotic and Christian duty, but something inside me resisted with a vengeance. I could not put myself in a position to harm someone over ideology. As my numerous appeals to the government for exemption from service were methodically turned down and my draft lottery number got closer to the top, my only choices seemed to be jail or Canada. I racked my brains trying to figure out why this terrible dilemma was in my life, finally coming up with the realization that I was being provided this gut-wrenching experience, as well as my general overall life confusion, as fodder for the great American novel, which I began to write with abandon.

My best friend, Bob, and I had received notices to have our induction physicals on the same day. Even though we were both appealing our draft status, the Army was proceeding to give everyone even remotely eligible mandatory examinations, anticipating that most appeals would be denied and therefore being able to expedite the induction process. Actually, it made good business sense, but at the time it seemed like just another unholy intrusion. The night before we were scheduled to go to the Oakland Armory to be medically processed along with several hundred other young men, Bob unexpectedly showed up at my apartment with a devilish smile and a large bucket of Colonel Sander's extra crispy chicken. He had devised a scheme to defeat "Big Brother." He would simply eat the chicken, bones and all, so that by the next day he'd be able to show blood in his stool and claim he had an ulcer or some sort of equally debilitating internal disorder. Squinting in disbelief, I told him I thought his plan was ridiculous; but, unaffected, he began chugging a few beers to build up his nerve and then started crunching away. As I drank a couple of cans myself while watching him eat and listening to his forced enthusiasm, the idea lost its initial repulsion and even began to sound almost plausible. A few scratched innards wasn't such a high price to pay to get out from under the Selective Service axe, but in the end (no pun intended) I just couldn't do that to my body. Believe it or not, his crazy plan worked.

For all the anxiety and anger that flowed through me during those long years of struggle with the establishment, it ended rather uneventfully. I had, quite by chance, been offered a job as a juvenile probation officer in Marin County and subsequently was granted an occupational deferment. The official notice came on an innocuous postcard one drizzly Tuesday morning. Unlike the movies, there was no band playing, no one to celebrate with, and not really anything to celebrate because the Vietnam war continued. I unexpectedly began to cry and spontaneously pounded my fists against the garage door a few times with the pent up frustration accumulated toward a faceless bureaucracy that had controlled my life for so long. "When will we learn?" I whispered. Without an answer, I went to class and then to work like I would do for many Tuesdays to come.

I may have ignored many aspects of life while fighting the draft, but it was love and sex (though maybe not in that order) in which I first renewed interest. With the great American novel finished, all I needed was that special person with whom to share my life. I'd simply send my manuscript off to the Scott Merrideth Literary Agency (considered to be the best at the time), set up housekeeping with the woman of whom I dreamed, and finally begin enjoying destiny's embrace. So, off went the book, and enter my first wife.

However, two minor problems developed with this particular plan. The first being that someone impersonating an agent from that prestigious New York firm returned my work with a so-called critique in which it was his inescapable conclusion that my novel was unpublishable. It wasn't that he didn't like my idea of having identical twin brothers switch lives to graphically illustrate the social injustice of the times; he did. However, he suggested that others in the literary community might possibly construe this idea as not completely original. He made reference to someone named Samuel Clemens, I think, but at that point in his correspondence I realized I had sent my manuscript to someone who couldn't possibly appreciate its true art. Unfortunately, future submittals to other agencies also failed to uncover a publisher or agent of discerning taste and intelligence. I realized this novel was ahead of its time and lovingly placed it in a prominent position on my bookshelf, where it would have to wait until society evolved a little further.

The second minor glitch to my life becoming perfect was the fact that my marriage quickly deteriorated. She was beautiful and we fell in love, which were, evidently, the two main requirements I had come up with for knowing my soulmate. Apparently, there were more things I wanted, though, because I found myself continually comparing her to Laura Petrie.

Everyone knew from the Dick Van Dyke Show that Laura Petrie was the standard role model for women, but for some reason my wife often acted like she had been raised by a completely different network. Like most people, I assume, we never really talked about our beliefs. We simply knew marriage was an agreement whereby the man would emulate Rob Petrie—playful, well-intentioned, and funny; and the woman would be like Laura—beautiful, devoted, supportive, naïvely sexy, intelligent, witty, resourceful, loyal, trustworthy, strong, sensual, generous, moral, talented, and loving. . . . And, I can state categorically that I was much more conscientious in fulfilling my matrimonial obligations than she was.

Although a little discouraged from the divorce and somewhat shaken that my immense love had not been able to change her into the one I needed, I consoled myself with the idea that I had learned a great deal from this false start and felt confident that I could now truly recognize the actual woman of my dreams, who was surely about to appear. In the meantime I could concentrate on my career in the civil service womb. Unfortunately, the more I moved up in this bureaucracy, the more politics and paperwork ensued, and the less fulfilling the job became. No matter how innovative I was or how much money I made, I couldn't shake the persistent feeling that I should be doing something else with my life.

When I resigned, however, I discovered rather rudely that I had a great deal of my self-worth wrapped up in the title and power afforded by that job. To make matters worse, I was going from an obvious "helping profession" into starting my own construction company whose only redeeming value was profit, which extracted some healthy guilt from my old but well-entrenched anti-establishment values. However, after some reflection, I concluded I must be going in the right direction, especially since this venture was the only convenient course available; and, on paper, it was a sure thing.

I would specialize in redwood-patio greenhouses and hot tubs. Wasn't Marin the peacock-feather capital of the world and reportedly to be the most self-indulgent community in the country? Who could have guessed that California was about to have the worst drought in recorded history? Certainly not me. Trying to sell hot tubs without the availability of water provided a challenge just slightly beyond even my considerable talents. This financial disaster caused me to again entertain the notion that just possibly there was something else I was supposed to be doing. Maybe I was the struggling great American novelist after all. So another book, this time a promising murder mystery, was begun while I pursued another profession.

It was time to return to doing something that helped society while endeavoring to change this country's money-grubbing system. I enrolled in a doctorate program with the laudable notion of becoming a respected professor. But, before classes could start, I happened to be offered a temporary position of managing a personnel department for a small computer company at a beginning salary that most tenured educators would kill for. "Certainly," I counseled myself, "a little more exposure to the varied practices of this corrupt business-oriented society could only serve to enhance my credibility as an educator later on." I didn't really count on enjoying working for the "enemy" as much as I did; and, once realized, it became apparent to me that my special contribution to changing society was obviously meant to be made from well within this decidedly decadent system. However, if this was the right path, it would be marked by the appearance of that special person, wouldn't it? So, I started looking around; she had to be close by. . . .

From the moment she dropped off her job application I was drawn to her. Samantha had a natural, country-girl quality about her, treating everyone as if they were next door neighbors. She was beautiful, of course, and I took the necessary time to make sure she was more like Laura Petrie than my first wife. She was also the most sexually amazing woman I had ever known, having up to ten orgasms to my one. (Yes, her's usually came in fairly rapid succession.) We lived together for awhile and, even though the relationship was confusing and tumultuous, we soon were married. In fact, our passionate, sexual bond was so strong that we even lived together a couple of times after the inevitable divorce, which I adamantly blamed on her misuse of alcohol and drugs, and she blamed on my lack of understanding. We went to counseling together a few times to no avail. The entire episode lasted about two years; and, in the end, I was just too angry with her for blowing thousands of dollars on chemicals and for not loving me enough to be who I wanted that I just refused to see her anymore. I didn't even know that she had moved away until months after the fact. However, I did acquire a hunch that she was equally incensed with me because she called me on the day she left, but not to tell me she was leaving: "I just want you to know, Rich, that, except for the first time we made love, I faked every orgasm I ever had with you."

I was speechless. Naturally, I had felt great every time we made love, believing that I could give her that much pleasure, but I had never thought of her multiple orgasms as a necessity for my enjoyment. She certainly could have accomplished the same positive effect on my self-esteem by faking just one or two each time. Since it made no sense, I, of course, took no time to look at anything about myself which may have precipitated such a strange (although commendable) effort on her part. After that unusual disclosure, I fully expected, and was more or less resigned, never to see her again.

Having learned yet another extremely painful, but obviously important lesson in relationships, I was now, beyond a doubt, ready for the real thing. My career progressed steadily through Silicon Valley, providing great financial incentives, but the work itself was rarely nourishing to my spirit. Training people to effectively manage and communicate had a degree of importance but hardly seemed like the major purpose for my life. But, since it allowed me to acquire property and toys, I simply moved on to another company when bored. In addition, I continued doing family counseling on a parttime basis, grateful that the State of California does not require therapists to practice what they preach. I figured I'd be able to get my life together and discover my ultimate contribution after I found my soulmate. I dated lots of women and even played house a couple of times, but "Ms. Right" stubbornly refused to appear in my life. So, I decided I'd give a little assist to fate's rather unpredictable timetable—I put an ad in the paper.

Now, that might sound like a crass and impersonal way to approach this delicate area, but quite frankly I was tired of leaving my ultimate happiness up to the capricious process of falling in love. This was a goal that needed a touch of logic. I had learned enough from all my previous romantic sorties that the perfect woman for me would, in addition to being Laura-like, be direct, independent, ambitious, and business-like. What better way to find someone like this than to advertise?

However, the first five women encountered through this method sorely tested my theory and almost convinced me to ignore the sixth and final respondent. We met for a drink, and within a few minutes it was obvious she was the "one." So, I breathed a sigh of relief and graciously accepted this overdue blessing from the Gods. In two months we were engaged. By the fourth month we were in the Bahamas to get married. By the eighth month we were divorced. So much for logic.

There was that one moment of hesitation, however, when I stood on our balcony of the Bahamian Hotel overlooking a tranquil turquoise Atlantic, trying to figure out why we had been unable to find a local minister of any faith willing to marry us. I actually contemplated the just possibility that maybe not all the Gods were smiling on this joint venture, but to even suggest such a possibility at that point seemed unreasonable and scary. It would have meant that I hadn't really learned anything from past relationships, and I would have been back to square one in trying to find that special person..

The failure of this third marriage and whatever important lesson it was teaching me meant only one thing—that's right, the one truly meant for me **had** to be close by! I was now in my late thirties. Certainly, I had learned what I needed to know about myself and was ready to get on with figuring out how to leave my footprint in life. In this frame of mind, I began to date Cindy, a gifted school teacher in Boulder Creek.

The captain's metallic voice brought me back to Continental flight 230. Expecting turbulence ahead, he was requesting that seat belts be fastened. I glanced over at Cher as I slowly stretched and shifted my weight in the chair. She was looking at a mesmerizing moon from the window of her fiancé's brother's apartment after having just made love to him. I could also see that a beleaguered stewardess was approaching my row in her methodical distribution of chicken or white-fish entrées. I waited until she was looking in my direction before smiling politely and briefly holding up my hand to indicate that I wasn't hungry. (I still did not want my possible last meal to be one served in cardboard and aluminum.) Besides, I was eager to get back to my own theater of exploration—I knew the turning point that was coming. . . .

       •   •   •

Though reluctant to talk too much about it, Cindy belonged to a small spiritual community called "Trees." She conscientiously attended their meetings several nights a week, which sometimes conflicted with my desire to be with her and engage in possibly less spiritual activities. Uncharacteristically, I invited myself along to one of these Friday night meetings after she admitted under persistent questioning that they were "kinda" open to the public.

The meeting was convened at the old Boulder Creek Recreation Club, a collection of several deteriorating buildings and two large stagnant puddled swimming pools. Although neglected for many years, this compound had been purchased by the community, an equal mixture of about twenty-five men and women of various ages, with the idea of purposefully growing algae and converting it into a nutritious and tasty food. They achieved half their goal in that the resulting dark green powder, usually mixed with fruit juice, contained enough nutrients to sustain a race horse; but, unfortunately, drinking the mixture could only be accomplished by firmly holding one's nose. Consequently, the property quickly reverted to a look that reflected this product liability. The service began in the large, low-ceilinged meeting room at 7 PM with everyone silently meditating in solemn postures on drab, worn couches until hearing a car pull up outside on the loose gravel, at which point a beautiful free form of chanting began.

Probably in his sixties and standing about six foot three with long grayish-blonde hair and a matching, well trimmed beard, Christone, the patriarch of the community, entered quietly from the back of the room. Walking to the front and sitting lotus style in a large, lamb-skin covered, elevated chair that allowed him an overview of the eighteen people gathered, he proceeded to give his thoughts on various aspects of spiritual life in a long discourse. When this was complete, his "students" began asking him questions about various problems they were encountering on their respective spiritual paths; and, after answering three or four, he left rather unceremoniously. The evening ended with tea and cookies and a chance to interact with Cindy's "family."

They all displayed a tremendous bond of love for and loyalty to each other; and, coming from the business world as I was, such warmth appeared as a very attractive oasis. There was a genuine desire in the community to help each other find happiness. When really stumped in that virtuous process, the source of all local wisdom, Christone, was right there to provide guidance. This was tantamount to studying Catholicism and having the Pope available as a tutor. Seeing that everyone in this community seemed to have a mission in their lives, I immediately recognized that a meaningful purpose was totally absent in my own life. Also, the community contained Cindy.

On the other hand, I was familiar with the Moonies. This caused me to maintain a healthy skepticism about the whole operation, even though everyone in the community's cluster of weathered houses a few miles from the recreation club appeared to live at a subsistence level, including Christone, aside from his one apparent luxury of a Cadillac. I spent much of my initial time trying to find the "scam," the hidden, selfish motive for the enterprise. I kept waiting for the suggestions that I should donate money, or even sell my house and physically move into the community. But, that never happened; and I was able to join at the "level one" status, living nearby on my own without any overt requirements that I change my life.

True to my previous form, Cindy and I soon broke up. When I delivered the bad news to her, all I could say was that I really didn't know what love was anymore. She was deeply hurt and had the audacity to think that I wasn't telling her the truth, not the whole truth anyway, which of course I denied. In all my previous relationships, once the decision was made to end them, I simply left and never had to deal with any of the issues. However, Cindy and I were attending a weekly class in the community on "creative conflict," a very effective communication process developed by none other than

Christone. Being confronted by Cindy and others in each successive class forced me, for the first time, to look at why I had withdrawn. Because there was a consensus in the group, except for me, that I was not being truthful, someone came up with the ridiculous idea that I should have intercourse with myself (Cindy might have termed this differently) by role playing my head talking to my heart. Self-consciously I agreed and awkwardly began a stupid little Gestalt game that quickly altered my perception of life.

As I stated out-loud what my head was thinking and then what my heart was feeling, I became acutely aware of the fact that my head ruled my heart, and had probably done so all my life. Hearing the comments from others during this schizo-phrenic exercise, it was also evident that my carefully crafted self-image was virtually transparent to all. Reluctantly, I began to see some areas in which I judged Cindy as not fitting the image of the woman meant for me. I had told her I loved her because I had needed a sexual relationship; and because, as usual, I wanted her to be the "one.," again believing she'd change for that love. Cindy remained very quiet until I had finished these remorseful revelations, but then came her devastating reaction of pain and anger. As she sobbingly poured out her heart, I felt she was speaking, finally, for every woman I had ever left—which was every woman I had ever loved.

This painful experience somehow gave my heart a stron-ger voice in my life; or maybe it's more accurate to say that I could now hear a different, more gentle voice. I began listening for it as I went through each day and, with a strange mixture of joy and anxiety, decided that I'd try, if I could, to let go of my life-consuming quest to find a soulmate and instead concentrate on what I was discovering within myself.

Shortly thereafter, a letter arrived from Samantha, my second ex-wife. She had joined an ACA group (Adult Children of Alcoholics), and one of the first steps they recommended was for her to go back and clean up her burned (or burning) bridges from the past. The letter went on to say she had two kids, a rocky second marriage, and was attending classes to become a medical assistant. I was surprised when reading her words, not just because she had contacted me out of the blue, but because my feelings for her were not dead. Although it was totally illogical, impractical and expensive, I impulsively called her and talked her into coming out with her kids for a week's visit. After putting the kids to bed each evening, we would sit by the fire and reminisce, taking turns asking each other, "Remember the time I did this, what was going on with you?" We literally went through our entire past relationship, giving to each other the understanding that had been so hard to offer at the time. I learned that she, along with her sister, had been sexually abused by their father. Consequently, and with the help of cocaine, she had spent much of her time and energy blocking out those painful years and her mistrust of men. We laughed and cried, and in the course of that week became friends. It was truly a healing experience; and, even though we felt like brother and sister, it was the first time I said "I love you" to a woman without an expectation that she look or act like Laura Petrie.

I hate it when I'm at the movies and I have to go to the bathroom, missing part of the plot. That's one advantage of watching my own production. I can stop it whenever the need arises. . . . Having attended to that insistent necessity and back in seat 23A, I saw that Cher was now at the opera, expressing her surprise and shock at seeing her father with a woman other than her mother. I closed my eyes to return to a somewhat less predictable movie where I was finally and unmistakably about to come face to face with the woman of my dreams. . . .

●   ●   ●

A more promising love cannot be found,
Than one fulfilling all our dreams,
Yet, such a love with glittered crown,
When possessed, is never what it seems.

Chapter Two

The Dance of Desire

Christone had decided our community would participate with another fledgling organization, One-Earth, in coordinating the next December 31 Peace Day project. About twenty of us were gathered for a two day planning session in a cluttered, crowded living room of an old summer cottage in Boulder Creek. We were taking turns introducing ourselves by sharing personal interests and commitments in the proposed venture. Suddenly, I found myself tense and my attention riveted as Dawyn (as in sunrise), one of the members of this other group, began to speak. Her words described a dedication to healing the world and bringing people together, but they were unnecessary for her passionate tone and spontaneous emotions instantly conveyed the love in her heart and her absolute trust in what she was doing. She had obviously been on a spiritual path for years. She lived four states away in Denver and, more than likely, had found her life partner already. After all, she was beautiful, witty, charming, articulate, purposeful, and, had I still been comparing, seemed more like Laura Petrie than Mary Tyler Moore. Even though my self-doubts told me there was no way a woman like this would see me as the "right one" for her, I could not take my eyes off her; and I self-consciously felt all could hear my pounding heart. Reverting to an adolescent clutz around beautiful women was nothing new for me, but this feeling was much more powerful and pervasive. However, not knowing what else to do, I quickly chalked it up to being horny. Also, because of my less than stellar track record in relationships, not to mention my perpetual confusion about life, I decided I would not try to engineer anything between us, truly leaving this one up to fate.

The next day during a working breakfast at a local restaurant we talked briefly; I thought this went pretty well in that I had made her laugh several times while managing not to trip or spill anything on her. However, my optimism lost its initial momentum when that evening she didn't even remember my name. I reluctantly took this as a sign to forget it, but my attraction to her was relentless.

Instead, over the next few weeks I wrestled my resistant attention toward the much labored and newly finished mystery novel. It was generating at least twice as much interest as my first literary undertaking, that is if such things can be measured by the volume of rejection slips. In the midst of this pursuit, the electronics company I worked for unexpectedly established a branch office in Denver, affording me the opportunity to participate in its grand opening celebration. Dawyn appeared pleased when I casually called to relate this coincidence, even inviting me to stay with her and help conduct a seminar she was giving.

Once there, I was, as expected, mesmerized by her loving nature and personal integrity, not to mention an angelic smile that seemed to effortlessly touch the heart of each person at this small gathering. I had met no one like her before. However, scattered throughout the house were several framed pictures of her posing with some bearded man, whom I hoped was a blood relative. So, in the best nonchalant posture and voice I could imitate, I casually asked if this guy was her "partner." I tried not to show my reaction to her response, but she had to have been comatose not to sense my disappointment.

Upon returning to California, I continued my self-exploration at my own, secure pace, again clinging to the notion that, when I was finally at some unspecified place of self-understanding, fate could and would provide that special relationship of which I dreamed. However, even if nothing came of it, I boldly resigned to tell Dawyn what I felt toward her, that is if the opportunity ever arose when we were alone.

It wasn't long before another three-day planning meeting was set, this time for Murrietta Hot Springs in Southern California. I knew she would be attending. I had heard welcomed though unconfirmed rumors that she was no longer in a relationship, so with hope I went. Although there was a definite friendliness between us, because of the constant meetings for the first two days of the conference, I was confined to surreptitiously staring at her while trying to act interested in the agenda.

Meals at this verdant facility were provided in a large rectangular cafeteria always filled with spicy aromas from an extensive hot buffet of creative vegetarian cuisine occupying the center isle and flanked by four long rows of narrow metal tables and chairs. At breakfast on the last day, the others in our group of fourteen finished quickly and, as if on cue, headed off to the reserved meeting room leaving Dawyn and me nibbling on our granola-covered yogurt. Although there was still a fair amount of clamor from the self-serve atmosphere around us, apparently the opportunity I thought I wanted had arrived— one of those moments equally charged with fear and hope.

"Dawyn," I said, turning to face her directly and taking her hands in mine, "I'm very attracted to you, and I'd like to pursue a relationship if that's possible." It wasn't the most romantic speech I'd ever delivered, probably because I was more concerned with getting it all out in one breath than I was with the actual words.

Quickly swallowing, she assumed a rather nervous smile and squeezed my hands in return, then casually looked over at the morning sun streaming in through a bank of uniform colonial windows that ran the entire length of the dining room.

After five or ten seconds of eternity, she said, "Is it hot in here to you?"

Needless to say, this was not the enthusiastic response I was hoping to elicit. I actually thought she was quickly, if not subtly, trying to change the subject to stall for time. Never was I so happy to have an impression proved wrong. Unbeknown to me, irreparable fissures had appeared in her current relationship and, for the week prior to the Murrietta meeting, she had gone to Mount Shasta to think things out. There, with the help of a friend and psychic healer, Dawyn experienced some premonitions of a new man coming into her life who would be her "life partner" in the work that she was to do, and she had cautiously suspected that this new fellow might be me. When I took her hands and made my declaration of love, such as it was, she felt her body temperature rise abruptly. To her this meant that either I was indeed the special man of her recent dreams or that she was simply having a predictable reaction to an inordinately hot cafeteria. Her question back to me had been asked to confirm or eliminate the latter alternative. Although unaware of her unique logic, I somehow had the presence of mind to come up with the right answer; and, once informed that the room temperature was normal, she embraced me and stated that she was attracted to me also.

Since her extrication from this other entanglement was not at all assured and knowing the emotional torment such a process can inflict, I came to the supportive assistance of my new friend by sending her a dozen roses and dropping in on her when in Denver on business, which, surprisingly enough, began to occur almost weekly.

Soon, there was the typical excitement when two people begin to fall in love. There was the added satisfaction and fun of charming all her friends. And, there was also the overwhelming rush of gratitude for her advanced spiritual way of life being my guide in this adventure. But, the most powerful aspect of our time together was maybe the simplest of all actions. Whenever she took my hand or looked into my eyes, my heart would overflow with emotion and at the same time be totally at peace. Consequently, making love took on a whole new dimension for me, unknown from anything I had experienced before, as if a sacred gift of divine design. I took this as an irrefutable omen that my soulmate relationship had finally materialized; and, because that was so apparent, I didn't even bother to mention it.

On my third visit, a few hours before my return flight she suggested that we meditate together. After lighting the obligatory candles and incense, we sat cross-legged, facing each other with eyes closed in a small, sunny room dedicated to that activity. Periodically, I would lift one eyelid ever so slightly to see if it was time to come out of "trance;" but while waiting I prepared myself for what I thought would be the next major step that was obviously about to occur in the courtship process, that of describing our past relationships with others. I had memorized a very believable explanation for the first marriage; and my planned recount of the second marriage was almost as good, certainly giving me the benefit of the doubt in its demise. But, the third marriage was a problem. There wasn't one explanation coming to mind that even I could believe. I finally resigned myself to a plea of temporary insanity. I knew she'd accept the insanity part—it was the "temporary" I was worried about. After about a half hour, when our eyes were again open, I took a deep breath as she took hold of my hands and began to talk.

"The only relationship I'm interested in is one of unconditional love."

This was definitely not the topic I had prepared for. I wasn't even sure what her announcement meant exactly, which scared me more than talking about those previous relationships. But, the way I felt about her at that moment was so expansive and non-conditional that I simply remained expressionless, hoping she would interpret my blank gaze as concurrence rather than fear.

Looking directly into my eyes and continuing with the gentlest of voices, she said, "Rich, I can see your being; I see the Christ in you."

I know that might sound blasphemous to some, but that was not her intent, nor was it taken that way. I remained motionless as tears involuntarily welled in my eyes and then rushed, with initial embarrassment, down my surprised face. Still looking into her understanding smile, I heard another voice, as if adding to her thoughts. . . but inexplicably it was coming from inside me.

"And, though you have forgotten me, I have not forgotten you."

This powerful internalized sound startled me, yet was somehow very familiar, like it belonged. There was no recrimination in it, no chastisement. It's tone actually carried a quality of compassion. I let my head drop and behind closed eyes began to see a kaleidoscope of the many blessings in the past that had graced my life to which I had previously been blind. Probably everyone experiences such a moment where they see how God has always been in their life; but even though it may be common, it didn't lessen the impact of giving me an unmistakably greater experience of myself. When I again looked up, Dawyn, too, was crying; we hugged. Never had I felt so close to and accepted by a woman. My heart was totally open and I wanted her to roam it freely. This experience of love and vulnerability was beyond any I had known.

Later, on the way to the airport, she rather nonchalantly asked about my past relationships. A quick tally of my marital misadventures caused her to burst out laughing. I was very relieved to realize that these miscues were not going to be a liability, but also felt a little let down at not having the opportunity to use my overly prepared explanations, at least the first two anyway.

We talked on the phone everyday. We wrote every other day. We gave each other meaningless, precious gifts and flowers every week. I wrote poems and songs, sent on tapes or left precariously on her answering machine. She would call back with her love of which I could not get enough. I was back in Denver every two weeks. She called me the greatest treasure of her life, a gift from God. I would wake up in the middle of the night to find her staring at me and caressing my face. She would simply say that she wanted to make sure it was all real, that she wasn't dreaming.

At dinner sometime during the second month she took a gold ring from her finger, a valued gift from her sister, and placed it on mine. "Right or wrong, I want us to live together," she said, a little embarrassed from being so direct; however the gesture was totally appropriate given our emotions. I had the ring she had given me duplicated and presented the "mate" to her as a surprise. Not long after that, a professional psychic friend of hers, trained somehow in such matters, married us on the "etheric level." To me the strange but painless ceremony symbolized, like the identical rings, our being soulmates. We stated our commitments to each other every morning so that each day was brand new, not bound by what we might have felt or said the day before.

It was now clear why I had gone through all my previous relationship pain. My painful persistence to find "the right one" had paid off at last; and it felt good to know that I had finally found, with Dawyn, that fated path upon which I would now discover my destiny. . . . But, in the spreading shadow of this bright moment of certainty lurked a sinister, dark fear—what would I do if for some reason I lost her? It was barely discernible, just small enough to ignore.

Suddenly, it was decision time. After a few sleepless nights, I acknowledged that true love was indeed beckoning to me. So, I gave notice on my job, sold everything I owned except what I could carry in my Toyota truck, and, suspending that vague but persistent apprehension in the center of my being, leaped into the abyss.

The well dressed lady in 23B began to laugh abruptly, and my eyes sprang open reflexively. Seeing that she was wearing headphones, I remembered where I was and again looked up at the small, tautly drawn canvass screen about twenty feet away. Cher was in the process of throwing her engagement ring back at her fiancé. I knew a happy ending was coming, at least for Cher. Again, I shifted my body position a little for comfort and, with a slight hesitation of facing the next reel of approaching memories, shut my eyes, which automatically signaled the imaginary projector to continue. . . .

•   •   •

As Dawyn and I merged, a coinciding event, aptly called Harmonic Convergence, occurred that was quite important from the New Age perspective. The Mayan calendar was entering its final twenty-six year cycle in mid-August, a metaphysical signal that the Earth was entering a new phase of evolution. A well known proponent of this phenomenon, and a friend of Dawyn's, was in the process of having "sacred stones" buried at various "sacred sites" throughout the world to enhance the new energy that would soon be radiating onto Earth. I really wasn't too clear on the actual mechanics of this unprecedented astronomical phenomenon; but, since Dawyn was helping to coordinate the event, I certainly wanted to do everything I could to make it a success. It also seemed appropriate to have some significant and arduous adventure mark the transition from my old life to this new one. So, scheduling two extra days onto my drive to Colorado, I volunteered to bury a handful of these strange ferrous icons designated for Mount Shasta.

I approached the climb with a healthy amount of arrogant naiveté and confidence; after all, what could happen to me? I was entering a predestined relationship. I packed my Walkman and several tapes so that I could listen to my favorite "hiking" music. Another small tape recorder was necessary so that I could make an on-going narration of this momentous trek for my beloved. In addition I had to bring my Minolta and three different lenses to visually record the Ascension. Since I planned to stay overnight at the top, I also packed several kinds of food, a gallon of water, a tent, a sleeping bag, parka and gloves, various items of extra clothing, rain gear, and toiletries. I even took my California driver's license with me to bury as a symbol of my letting go of the past.

The day before my planned departure, I arrived in the city of Mount Shasta to pick up the "sacred stones" from a local, stained glass artisan who was caretaking them. Naturally shaped in the form of a two-inch tetrahedron (pyramid), each of the twelve, exquisite stones had a lava-like texture and color. The excited artist asked if I'd consider burying one of his own personal crystals along with these stones, which of course I agreed to do. There were three other people visiting in his house at the time and each, upon learning of my planned endeavor, asked if they could also contribute a special crystal. I again agreed to without much thought. However, as news spread throughout this small but well-connected town over the next couple of hours, the donation requests continued until I had at least ten additional pounds of unplanned freight to tote.

I was somewhat amused by the similar demeanor of these sincere people as they placed in my hands their precious clear prisms, as if entrusting me with a pet, or in some cases their child. One very serious man with great humility handed me a yellowish, opaque quartz slab that weighed at least five pounds just by itself. He said it was ancient and that for quite some time it had been telling him it wanted to go back to the Earth to finish its work. I was curious as to what that chore might be but decided it best not to ask a question that would reveal my ignorance in this area, instead excusing myself while I could still lift my now bulging pack.

As I was about to drive off, Dawyn's healer-friend took me aside and presented me with a beautiful red, silk pouch. In it she had placed an amethyst crystal, some ginseng root, a few kernels of ancient Hopi corn, two eagle feathers to guide me during the day, and two owl feathers to guide me at night. With her dark, intense eyes searching my face, she also expressed concern that I was going to stay overnight on the mountain. She said even experienced climbers don't usually stay on Shasta's summit. I paid little attention to the words I felt were obviously coming from a strong maternal nature. I simply smiled and hugged her, appreciating her caring. With that, I drove to the trailhead to spend the night.

Awaking early and greeted by another beautiful July morning, I tossed the tent back into the truck, knowing I wouldn't need it. It took three awkward tries before I succeeded in swinging the straining, red nylon backpack into proper position on my unsuspecting shoulders. Quickly taking one last look around out of habit, I inhaled deeply and headed up the dusty path amidst stately firs and the ever-present patches of manzanita. Two other climbers, busily assembling their own gear in the parking lot, paused briefly to exchange uncertain, excited smiles before the forest gathered me in. Rounding the first bend in silence, I noticed my attitude toward the climb had sobered. With all the personal possessions and good wishes given to me by so many people, I didn't feel I was doing this entirely solo anymore; and I began to entertain the notion that just possibly there was some significance to this action beyond its intended use of impressing Dawyn.

There are really no trails on Shasta above the nine-thousand-foot level because, being of volcanic origin, the mountain is covered by loose shale and stone. The best way to climb it, I was assured by the mountaineering equipment rental people, was by using crampons on the semi-permanent ice pack, which, like frozen fingers, lay deep in the many gullies on the south face, snaking up to connect with the large snowy blanket that covers most of the upper elevations.

Traversing the ice in this manner proved to be much more scary than difficult; however, I totally over-estimated my strength for that altitude, especially with the weight of my cargo. After ten hours of exhaustive climbing in which I didn't have the energy to take even one picture, I found myself about fifteen hundred feet below the summit at a ridge just to the east of the Red Banks, a massive out-cropping of crumbling, earth-colored rocks. From this spot on the mountain I could see both the south slope, which I had just come up, and the east slope, which was completely covered by the Konwakiton and Wintum glaciers until they gave way to the dark green of the timber line miles below.

Since the sun was descending quickly, it seemed unlikely that I was going to reach the pinnacle. This prospect was a relief to my tired body but also produced in me a strong sense of failure. I had agreed to bury the stones "on top" of Shasta. Of course, who was going to know? And besides, all around me were loose rocks and shale that were not conducive at all to the burial ceremony I had pictured. In addition, for some odd reason it was starting to get cold. If I hurried, I knew I could make it back down to the tree line where there was appropriate terrain for burying and where it would also be a little warmer. Surprisingly, and for some unknown reason, integrity, not my most frequent companion in the past, won out; and I decided it was somehow important to follow through on what I had said I'd do.

Because of the large rock and ice formations higher up, the only path open to me that led in the direction of the summit was a narrow ledge about four feet in width starting a few feet below me on the eastern slope and then winding out of sight to my left just above the glacier's rim. I proceeded cautiously because of the many loose rocks. Slipping off the ledge would have resulted in only a ten or fifteen foot fall; however, landing on that smooth, steep ice pack would have initiated a rather menacing five-mile slide. I wrongly assumed this narrow shelf provided access to the plateau above the cliffs because, once around the curve of the mountain, it ended abruptly without any way for a single climber to scale higher. The only route to the top now was to backtrack down the south slope and hunt for a opening through the ice-covered crevices of the Red Banks. Understandably discouraged and slowly plodding back along the ledge, I noticed a slight indentation in the cliff wall, almost in the shape of a lounge chair that would allow someone to lean back and be somewhat protected from the elements. I somehow instantly "knew" this was the place to bury the stones and quickly unbuckled my pack, letting it swing to the ground with a thud. I looked around proudly at the official "sacred site" I had discovered, pleasantly surprised to realize my psychic abilities evidently get better with fatigue.

As promised, when 11 PM came I quickly buried the stones under several clumps of barely liftable shale, climbed into my sleeping bag, pulled it over my head, and began the impossible task of trying to ignore my solid granite bed. After a while I restlessly looked at my watch; it was exactly midnight. I was extremely cold and, strangely enough, damp. Sticking my head out to see if those strange, blinking stars were still there, I saw something that quickly jerked me into a sitting position. It was snowing! I was actually covered by a good inch of wet powder that was in the process of melting from my body heat and soaking into my sleeping bag.

Mustering my rarely used resourcefulness, I realized that if I put my rain gear on over my clothes the moisture seeping into the sleeping bag wouldn't get me wet, yet I would still be afforded its warmth. Grabbing my pack, I hurriedly located the tightly folded plastic poncho and pants; and, as I began to spread them out, they disintegrated into shreds, evidently melted by the sun on the way up. Okay, plan B. Unfortunately, plan B required the use of the tent, which was at that very moment comfortably residing in the dry cab of my truck.

Okay, plan C. I'd head back down the mountain. With that in mind, I began to assess my situation carefully. Over the ridge to my right, I could see and hear the evidence of what gave every appearance of being a full blown blizzard. There was no way I could make it down over the ice and rocks in the dark without a fair likelihood of twisting an ankle, breaking a leg, and getting lost. Okay, plan D. I pulled the sleeping bag back over my head and began to swear.

For the next two hours I was in a state of total disbelief. How could this be happening? I wasn't at all prepared for a snow storm, and Dawyn and I had only enjoyed a few weeks together. Someone had made a mistake here. I shouldn't even have been on this ungrateful mountain. I was really only doing it as a favor to my new (and now questionable) friends who believed in Harmonic Convergence. . . .

At about 3 AM I took another hopeful peek out of my soggy cocoon. The snowing had slowed considerably as the clouds partially lifted, inviting a three quarter moon to sprinkle its pale light across the entire eastern panorama. For miles in all directions, everything was covered with a pristine white cloth of glistening stillness. I sat transfixed, sensing Shasta's eternal partnership with the Universe. Until that moment I would have described myself as being fairly conservative and eminently logical, but rising up within me was the unnerving certainty that I was not alone.

In another few minutes the clouds recollected and the snow quickly returned, along with my apprehension. Dejectedly, I located my tape recorder, narrated a detailed description of my forsaken situation (expletives included), and dramatically dictated a last will and testament, which included an impassioned farewell to Dawyn. . . . By 6 AM the wind had increased the chill factor significantly. Through the swirling snow, I could only see about thirty or forty feet in any direction, and ice had formed on the sleeping bag as well as on all the rocks around me. My body was numb and shivering, but I convinced myself that the best thing to do was stay put. It had been ninety degrees for the whole prior week, for Pete's sake. This storm couldn't last too long. I briefly admonished myself for not registering my name and planned route with the park rangers, but figured Dawyn's friend would call them when I didn't show up at her house as expected. In depressed resignation, I started again to pull the sleeping bag up over my head when I heard a distinct commanding voice.

"It's time to go."

Without looking around to see where it was coming from, I simply took it as a definite sign to leave and just hoped that it meant back to civilization rather than the "great beyond." My mind was still trying to debate the issue and figure out a way to gather and carry my copious equipment when I realized I had already scrambled up the steep incline at the far end of the ledge, leaving all my gear where it lay, and was heading for the crest of the ridge that led to the south slope. Once on the other side, the howling wind caught me from behind with tremendous force. Disoriented, I was slipping with every step, creating constant, small avalanches that carried me haphazardly and painfully on my butt for several bumpy yards before I could stop myself by painfully digging my arms into the loose shale. I grabbed onto a large rock nearby, closed my eyes and waited, letting sticky snow flakes collect on my face like cold finger tips. Part of me was still back on the ledge trying to make logical decisions, but within a few minutes my alertness returned.

It took four perilous hours to reach the relative safety of the marked trail. As I slowly shuffled past the historic stone cabin just below the timberline, a young woman with a child of about seven emerged. When the mother saw me, she instinctively grabbed for her child in a protective gesture. I was puzzled by their fright until I let my head drop and observed that I was encrusted with snow and ice, as though a disgruntled escapee from a botched cryogenics experiment. Amused by the situation and relieved to see other people, I began laughing, which immediately assuaged their concern. Having also been caught unprepared by the storm, the mother was glad to see someone else and began chatting as we walked. She casually mentioned that snowing was nature's way of purifying things. With that I stopped to look back at the mountain, still shrouded in the swirling clouds, and thought about it's moon lit, shimmering grandeur of the night before, and of the sacred stones it had received just before the unexpected storm. Although it was confusing and stretched my ability to accept the unusual, somehow I felt like it all had happened according to some unwritten script.

"Please bring your seat to a full, up-right position." I think the stewardess had to ask it twice before I realized where I was and opened my eyes. She smiled knowingly and continued on her rounds as I complied with her perfunctory request. I lifted the noisy window shade in time to see the familiar silhouette of Stapleton Airport just twisting from view as we circled in the usual holding pattern, but quickly shut my eyes again, wanting to watch my movie as long as I could. . . .

●   ●   ●

Delightfully, the honeymoon began about ten minutes after I pulled up in front of her house. I was prepared for it to last forever, as in my mind it was designed, but such was not the case.

After a couple months, a weekend camping trip materialized with some friends, James and Barbara, authors who were widely considered to have access to the "higher" levels of consciousness and therefore, I anticipated, would be of invaluable assistance in furthering my spiritual education. The campsite was isolated and beautiful, high on a rugged granite cliff overlooking a lazy, pastoral valley. After building a campfire, we all settled down in a casual circle. James continued talking about his books and philosophy, occasionally stopping to play an unfamiliar melody on a strange looking flute. At one point, while emphasizing how we all create our own limitations which then prevent us from seeing that we really have no limits, he decided to crudely illustrate this truth by boldly sticking his tongue in Barbara's nose and then into one of Dawyn's nostrils. I initially thought this strange but also knew that great insights often come from unexpected events. However, when he looked over at me, I politely and humorously declined his unspoken invitation to release my traditional conditioning around such invasions. Not to be dissuaded, he jerked forward and rather forcefully grabbed the back of my head, pulling me close and kissing me on the lips.

I was shocked, though I must say, my surprise was mixed with a certain amount of curiosity. I had not been kissed like that by a man before and, having never even come close to initiating such an action, I thought I should at least evaluate the experience. Since he had a mustache very similar to mine, my first reaction was an instant appreciation for all the women I had made love with who had somehow been able to control their tickle reflex. Doing a quick emotional inventory, I also gratefully discovered that my two imagined worst fears associated with kissing a man had not materialized—I didn't feel an overwhelming desire to kill him, nor did I have an erection. Other than some self-conscious awkwardness, it was like shaking hands. I leaned back not knowing what to say; however, my expression must have revealed me, as James developed a big grin of what looked like satisfaction for having exposed my limits. He then gave Dawyn a kiss accompanied with what I perceived as a rather passionate embrace.

At this point I began impatiently waiting for the insight or revelation that would be worth the rage of tremendous jealousy that was slowly, but inexorably, beginning to flood through me. After a minute or two, I did what any rational person on the spiritual path would do in this situation; I quickly evaluated his physical strength and ascertained that, if I was quick, I could probably express my rushing anger in a most appropriate and demonstrable way. I would simply expose James's limits with regard to flying by launching him off the nearby cliff. . . . But, I hesitated. Dawyn seemed compliant with what was happening. Couldn't she see that his intent had less to do with reaching the realms of higher consciousness than achieving physical gratification? Or was she just being her sweet, nurturing self, not wanting to hurt his feelings by resisting? As my still unacknowledged dread of losing her completed it's coup of my faculties, I firmly concluded that I was not over-reacting. But, regardless, I had vowed to love her unconditionally. How was I to reconcile what I felt like doing to James with what I had committed to be with Dawyn?

With this internal war raging, I was only peripherally aware of Barbara who seemed actively engaged in a nervous philosophic statement directed toward James in what appeared to be an unsuccessful attempt to entice him into talking again. So, she turned her attention toward me, expressing the hopeful axiom that just because two people are kissing it doesn't mean that the primary relationships with their respective partners are in danger. She then attempted to give me a kiss; I guess to prove her point.

"There must be something here I'm missing," I mentally scrambled in a vain attempt to convince myself, as every cell in my body now screamed for action. But Dawyn was my spiritual guide; and James was someone she looked up to, along with many others, as a great teacher. Where was the hidden lesson or meaning in this gnawing situation that could assist me to a higher level of personal understanding? It was extremely distressing to realize that evidently I was not as far along the path of enlightenment as I had assumed.

After what seemed like an appropriate, but agonizingly long period of time, I stated, in a calm and resolute tone, I didn't feel comfortable, and got up to leave. Dawyn, with a startled look, immediately grabbed my arm and asked that I stay.

James responded with what sounded like a question, "We're all part of the same family?" Now he was the one looking surprised.

"I realize we are all family, James," I said, "but, I just don't have the desire to make love with all my relatives."

I guess my actions were not real conducive for the expansion of limits, as an uneasy quiet descended over the four of us. We huddled there, each in our own thoughts, looking up at the stars. . . . After a little while Dawyn and I went off to be by ourselves. She quickly insisted that it was never her intention to make love with James; they were only being close to one another and "snuggling". I asked if she could define for me the point at which snuggling stopped and making love started. She shrugged and, instead, described for me her certainty of having a Karmic connection with James. Somewhere in a past life or in the etheric dimensions she had made an agreement with James to connect at this time. She felt that she and James were meant to do something important together, probably for the world or for each other's personal growth. She believed she might have many such Karmic connections and agreements to fulfill with other people in this lifetime. In addition she explained that one of the main indicators for these Karmic contracts was often a physical attraction. This was the Universe's way of letting people about such agreements.

I'm sure she went on sharing many other thoughts and feelings with the desire to have me understand her truth, but I was no longer listening. I wondered why she hadn't shared this with me before now. I never even considered the possibility that maybe she had and for some reason I hadn't heard. I only knew that our relationship most certainly fell into this category of Karmic arrangements, but I felt no such fated directives toward others. The churning concern of how she was going to keep her commitments to me and also honor this Karmic directive devoured all other thoughts. I did not see that my immense fear of losing her now completely surrounded my perceptions and emotions like a dark shroud.

The next morning the four of us headed back to town. No one mentioned the incident, and conversation was tentative. Something seemed subtly changed between Dawyn and myself. As the car wound through the scenic foothills into Boulder, I thought I sensed a question in her mind not being asked, maybe even the same unwanted question I had—would our love be strong enough? It was a question that for some reason I could not voice.

As the weeks passed, I sought reassurance in other, more tangible ways. It became logically obvious to me that if our relationship could maintain the same intensity and types of activities as it had when we fell in love, I would have nothing to worry about. So, naturally if a few days went by and we hadn't, for instance, made love, I felt obliged to find out why the relationship was on the decline. The first few times, she merely insisted I was mistaken, which was, of course, what I wanted to hear. But after awhile, my attempts to reconstruct a "newly wed pattern" to our life were met with the annoyed response, "Why can't we just enjoy what we have instead of constantly dwelling on the past?" However, this request made no sense to me because our current relationship was no longer the stuff of which dreams are made.

In concealed desperation, I continued "surprising" Dawyn with cards and flowers each week, hoping that these gifts would convince her that I loved her and pleasantly persuade her to return to the frequency and method of expressing love in the way two people who are meant to be together should. I bought a hot tub for the backyard, my subtle attempt for us to be together in a sensual way at the end of each day; but we ended up using it separately. Unaware of the recluse I had become, attempting to map out new strategies in my downstairs office, I silently accused her of withdrawing deeper into herself and into a separate life. Even when we did manage to have fun, those times were increasingly cut short by my wondering how long it would last. Her daily activities of joyfully giving to and helping others, once a source of inspiration to me, I now perceived as a convenient means of avoiding the painful tension that hung around us like an albatross. Focusing only on what I wasn't receiving from her, I refused to accept whatever was offered. Firmly in the righteous grip of my unseen fear, I began to hate the very one I had promised to love forever.

Within a few months, the intrusive weariness of unresolved perceptions had done their damage as our spontaneity, openness, humor, and love making completely eroded. Our previous commitments of love and devotion to each other, which had been such a bonding source of comfort and enjoyment in the beginning, were fading memories. And worst of all, back then in the comfort of our acknowledged need for each other, I had been able to display a very independent, spontaneous, and witty demeanor. Now, I found myself unwilling to be the person with whom she had fallen in love. I missed being that person, and I blamed her. If she'd just love me like she used to, I could be free to be myself again—I could be happy.

It was a Thursday, I believe, and we had been living together for not quite a year. Dawyn was to leave the next day for a conference in England, and I was off to the self-empowerment seminar in Boston. I asked her to sit with me in the backyard and talk. She agreed without emotion. I asked her what the ideal primary relationship would be for her. She said it would be one where both people loved each other unconditionally and loved all others, too; one that was fun, expressive, dynamic, spontaneous, and not bogged down in trying to make it fit old pictures; one that was purposeful in helping to bring about the transformation of world conscious-ness; and one in which both people supported each other in doing what they came here to do. Her words were very beautiful to me, as were all the words she shared from her heart. I replied that I wanted exactly the same thing but that I really didn't experience her putting much energy into our relationship to make it into what she had described. She looked away in thought for a minute and then agreed with that assessment, adding that she didn't know why her desire had waned but that she'd think about it in England.

As we lay in bed that night, we talked briefly about our approaching respective trips. She appeared as happy and vivacious as I'd ever seen. There was no indication of conflict in her world. Spurred by a jealous curiosity, I said, "Life is like a candy store to you, isn't it?"

She paused, momentarily letting go of whatever else she may have been thinking about, and then smiled. "I suppose in a way it is. What's wrong with that?" she answered with confidence.

Nothing more was said between us as we both drifted into separate dreams. No, there was nothing so terribly wrong with living life as if it were a candy store. I pictured Dawyn, her favorite confections being the Karma covered ones, those relationships filled with predestined ingredients that she could relish as long as that divine-flavored elixir she liked remained. Actually, a candy store philosophy of life sounded pretty inviting, unless one happened to be the candy that's lost its Karma.

"On behalf of Continental Airlines, I'd like to welcome you to. . . ."

Traffic was light this weeknight, and it only took a few minutes to get home by cab from the airport. The house Dawyn and I shared was as empty as it was depressing. She wasn't due back from England for days. Just wanting to be with nature, I quickly restocked my suitcase and jumped in my pickup truck. The Colorado Rockies, of course, were very convenient, but for some reason I found myself skirting by them through the darkness to head north on US-25 toward Wyoming. I wasn't tired; in fact, I wanted to continue my mental wandering for clues.

From all the successful and enlightened people I had encountered and studied during my life, surely there were some important truths that lay hidden in these memories and experiences. I briefly pictured Werner Erhart and various other polyester gurus I had long ago followed in hopes they could give me the truth (or, more accurately, sell it to me). But, as it turned out, my life remained circular even with their truths.

As the night shadows rushed passed, I took a deep breath and let it escape as a long sigh. I really didn't know where I was going with all this introspection. I only knew where I wasn't going; I wasn't going to let Dawyn give me any more confusion and pain. (It's amazing how brave we can feel when the object of our fear is eight thousand miles away.) But, of all the events I could have recalled from my life, why these? The situations jumping out at me were the painful, awkward ones where I just couldn't do anything right. I wasn't proud of my failed relationships or my dissatisfying career or that in general I just never seemed to accept life. Every road I had taken, no matter how important or attractive it was labeled, seemed to eventually lead in circles and left me empty. It was like I'd always been on a quest of some sort; I had always thought it was to find a soulmate and then my destiny, but now I wasn't sure what I had been searching for. . . .

•   •   •

Seeking the answer we lend our attention
To all who shout upon the wind,
But when at last arriving for our redemption,
It always seems comes from within.

Chapter Three

The Voice of Knowing

As dawn broke in Wyoming, I found myself standing expectantly on the side of the road about ten miles north of Jackson
Hole, gazing at the rugged, snow draped spires of the Grand
Tetons. Although it was beautiful and pleasing to my beleaguered spirit, other than knowing that I wanted to just get away
I had only a slight and uncollected premonition as to why I was
there.

None of the park trails was accessible because of the
extensive Spring snowpack, so I spent a couple of days hiking
off the beaten path on the lower elevation of the eastern
plateau. Resting on a small knoll facing west and watching a
flock of geese in "V" formation fly noisily overhead toward
the northern horizon, my eye caught the jagged, granite slopes
and followed them down where they gave way to a broad,
grassy valley, ribboned with the winding, ancient trails carved
by countless elk and caribou following their migratory destinies.
How was it that nature can paint such an intricate and complex
scene in perfect harmony, yet my life remained a mysterious
portrait of confusion? Even those distant honking geese,
annoyingly, knew exactly where they were going.

But, then it came to me like a brilliant bolt of mental
lightning. Reviewing the movie of my life had shown me that
the truth I sought was not in my past as much as my future. The
secrets to my destiny, and hopefully that special person, really

were out there; I just hadn't looked in the right places. I would go to the Great Pyramid of Cheops of which I had heard others, including Dawyn, recall mysterious and meaningful experiences. I would go to India and find a real guru to learn of that ascetic wisdom. I would climb Ayers Rock and visit the truly sacred sites of the Earth to acquire their higher connection with the Universe. In somewhat similar fashions even Warner and Christone had described finding their teachers and their destinies. Surely such a pilgrimage would reveal **my** truth. . . . Besides, if I was going to die, why not on an adventure of purpose?

After two more days of camping where I began planning this sacred and necessary course of action, I learned from one of the locals in Jackson Hole, after the customary amount of idle conversation, of a nearby hot springs. This was intriguing because I hadn't heard of any being in the area and the weather was certainly cold enough to warrant investigation. After about a half hour of driving on back roads and thinking I was lost more than once, I spotted a small, marshy area, with tall reeds and what looked like it could be a pond. Maybe in Wyoming this was a hot springs, but in reality it was more of a tepid bog. Gas of some type was bubbling up through the water, heating it enough to keep from freezing. No more than two feet deep and about a hundred feet in circumference, the pond was brightly painted in lime green by long swirls of algae and supported a healthy chorus of frogs and birds that were well-camouflaged but very excited upon my arrival. The water really wasn't warm enough to entice me, but I maneuvered my way out onto a dry section of marsh in the middle and sat cross-legged in my brown and white serape to let my thoughts go in meditation, an introspective practice I now did regularly, although never quite sure if correctly. As I closed my eyes and took a few deep breaths, I was suddenly back at a campfire that had provided warmth many years before.

It was at Turtlehead Lake, about twenty miles south of Big Bend in the California Sierras, right after I had left my probation officer's job and my first wife—another time of confusion and pain. That particular lake wasn't plotted on the forest service's topographical charts, so I had named it myself in honor of the prominent rock so shaped along its shore. After a quick ceremony of drawing it on the appropriate map, I was sitting cross-legged by the fire with my eyes closed, probably wondering "why me?", when I heard a distant but distinct snap of a twig. It sounded as if it were about fifty feet behind me and to the right. I thought it was highly unlikely to be another camper, since I hadn't seen anybody else in several days and it was definitely too dark for anyone to be out hiking, especially off the trail. Two snaps later, each a little closer, brought me to the point of decision: "Do I trust in God, or the Universe, or nature, or whoever's responsible for this whole thing, or do I open my eyes and turn to protect myself, if necessary, like any rational human being?"

Somehow, I was able to continue my stoic introspection through at least another dozen, ominous snaps until the last one was no more than a few feet in front of me, then silence. When I could stand the suspense no longer, I opened my eyes and froze. Before me was the soft gaze of a large brown-eyed buck, its six-pointed antlered head lowered to my level, surprisingly, right over the campfire. I was gripped by two impulses at once. My fear could see nothing but huge, formidable antlers and wanted to get the hell out of there; but my curiosity, probably stimulated by Carlos Castaneda's books about "allies," wanted to connect with it in some meaningful way. After a minute or two, it turned and walked back into the night. . . .

The sharp crackling sound of several fist-sized rocks bouncing down the steep incline about twenty-five yards to my right hurriedly brought me back to the Wyoming hot springs. I smiled from the déjá vu, again debating whether to open my eyes or trust the Universe. Just when I had made up my mind on the latter, more rocks began tumbling in the same area and persisted for several minutes. Resisting the incredible impulse to turn and face this noisy intruder, I pictured the springs and the surrounding area in my mind's eye. The embankment, now being traversed by something clumsily announcing its presence, ended about fifty feet or so from the springs where the ground became flat with intermittent patches of thick grass. Once on this level area, whatever it was probably wouldn't make much noise, I figured. However, after the rocks stopped their clamor, I continued to hear a variety of muffled sounds, none of which I recognized, coming from several locations at the edge of the springs. Something was obviously moving around the pond but unwilling or unconcerned about venturing to the middle where I was.

Finally allowing my eyes to open, I was instantly seized with startled elation. Encircling the springs was a herd of at least fifty buffalo, some now eyeing me cautiously as I turned my head and shoulders to view this remarkable sight; but most calmly sipping water or nibbling vegetation. Common sense told me that if I remained still everything would be fine, which proved true for the next few minutes of absolute joy. As most of the herd began to slowly wander back toward the rocky incline, three or four large males remained at the water's edge as if positioning themselves between me and the others.

One in particular seemed to be staring at me intently; and, as I returned his gaze, a peculiar feeling descended. The situation began to lose all sense of threat for me, and I heard a distinct voice in a strong, low tone say, "Walk with me." My ears couldn't quite place the sound, though the voice was definitely familiar; and my head swiveled reflexively in both directions before I realized that it was actually inside my head. With it came the unmistakable impression that I had been at this location or in this setting many times before, though such a notion was quite impossible. I also knew, again with a strange sense of surety, that I could walk among these buffalo without harm.

I stood up slowly, catching the attention of several more shaggy males. As I crossed the shallowest strip of marsh to solid ground with deliberate steps, the three buffalo closest to the water bolted back about thirty feet, kicking up soft, short-lived puffs of reddish dust in their haste. Now the entire herd was alert and fixed on the strange figure moving steadily · toward them. A few females with calves scurried up the far incline, only to pause at the top and look back with curiosity. The male nearest me turned his massive head slightly to face me squarely and resumed an unblinking, proud stare. I stopped my approach about ten feet from him and only then noticed that I was smiling. His magnificent horns were level with my chest, and the top of his shoulder girth appeared to be over six feet from the ground. His dark nostrils twitched as if trying to smell my intent. At last, he snorted loudly and cautiously lowered his head to resume nibbling a thick clump of grass. As I resumed my cautious approach, he deftly moved to one side, maneuvering his body so that I was always in his sight. At this point all of the herd returned to lunching while maintaining a steady southerly meandering. If I got within arm's length of any particular animal, it would nimbly trot a few steps to one side and watch me until I had walked by. I delighted in this ancient, choreographed dance for some distance over the rocky knolls until the descending curtain of darkness brought it to a close. I returned to the springs elated and, in the twilight's chill, paused to let my euphoric gratitude and wonder silently spill out over this magical place.

I didn't understand what had just happened, nor did I have an explanation for the deer at Turtlehead Lake, or the eerie events on Mount Shasta. In the past my mind had always been able to come up with plausible explanations or simply ignore strange things like these. But here I was asking for the truth to be revealed about my life and, instead, encountering these uncanny happenings. I wondered if God or the Universe was trying to tell me something, but I really didn't want to believe in anything "super-natural." Yet, at the same time I was very tired of my general confusion and was finding it extremely hard to continue resisting those things that didn't fit my more traditional beliefs. With a heavy sigh I just smiled with gratitude for such a marvelous day.

"No thanks is necessary."

My eyes opened wide with anticipation as I recognized the tone as having been the same voice that had invited me to walk with the buffalo. But this time I felt a strong tremor of fear, wondering if the stress of my crumbling life was driving me crazy.

"No, you're not going crazy. You're just talking to yourself."

"Well, that's dumb," I said in thought. "If I were going crazy, of course I'd tell myself I wasn't. . . . I think I've talked to myself before, and this definitely doesn't feel like just talking to myself," my silent logic continued.

"You 'think' you've talked to yourself before! You talk to yourself all the time; everyone does. You're just used to being in control of both sides of the conversation."

I began slowly shaking my head in disbelief and exhaled a nervous, forced laugh.

"Take this morning for example. You were practicing what you were going to say to Dawyn when she gets back, and then you'd respond to yourself as if you were Dawyn trying to anticipate what she'd say, right?"

I felt at a distinct disadvantage in this exchange and more than a little foolish, even though there was something very safe about the voice's intimate tone. However, I concluded it best to just ignore this dialogue and head back to the truck to begin the long drive home, which I began at a brisk walk.

"You don't need to answer. We both know it's true. You think by talking to yourself you can be objective, but unfortunately you only say what you want to hear. I on the other hand will be painfully honest with you."

"Oh, so you're my voice of honesty and any other internal voices I hear will be self-deceptive, eh?" I said aloud, sticking my hands in my jean pockets rather defiantly and picking up my pace.

"Not deceptive as much as confusing. For example in your current yearning to discover the truth and claim your destiny you have begun to plan a pilgrimage of enlightenment. . ."

My eyes narrowed from this intrusion of my thoughts, and I could feel my shoulders becoming rigid.

". . . that includes collecting the knowledge of the Pyramids, connecting with God at so-called sacred sites of the world, and finding a Hindu Holyman for a guru. This of course is a very ambitious and noble undertaking, and no doubt you will gain much from it. . . but is it really as right for you as it so obviously appears?"

For some reason I began to trot and feigned a growing interest in something off in the distance.

"It does offer adventure, which you like. It affords the opportunity to get your mind off your current dilemma. And, it's also something with which Dawyn might just possibly be impressed."

Reaching the truck, I hopped up to sit on the front fender, propping my feet on the tarnished bumper and glancing around quickly in all directions. I was feeling naked, and its words were like a very cold draft.

"The voices you listened to in making this decision all came from your desire to ease your current emotional pain."

"That may be partly true," I said self-consciously in rebuttal, "but there's also just good plain logic behind it. My current life is not bringing me in contact with any great teachers, and obviously there's value in such a pilgrimage because some pretty high beings have taken similar paths." (Besides, I had to defend this decision; it was the only plan of action I had other than suicide.)

"Ah, the voice of logic. Let me remind you of something that you already know, the certainty of which did not come to you through admirable reasoning. . . ."

I took a deep breath and, glad that no one was around to witness this mental "breakdown," slightly lowered my head in anticipation.

"The Universe has spent countless centuries directing its energy to form the billions of stars and planets. . . ."

I glanced up reflexively at the emerging night sky.

"It has taken hundreds of millions of years to sculpt this beautiful Earth. It has spent at least a million years creating an unbroken connection of living tissue in order to form your body and give you the mysterious miracle of life that you now experience. It is highly unlikely that all of this has been done without some reason, without some purpose. And, it is just as unlikely that the Universe would let your understanding of its true nature and your contribution to its purpose be solely dependent on reading a specific book, or visiting a particular piece of land, or running into exactly the right teacher."

Momentarily, my body shivered as a jolting chill run up my spine, but not just from the words, although I found them powerful. I suddenly realized this was also the voice I had heard on Mount Shasta. . . and when meditating with Dawyn. . . .

"The Universe is not so secretive that it allows interpretation by only a select few. As it is with each, you have been born with the inherent ability to discover for yourself all its truths."

I remained motionless, captured by these thoughts.

"As for your pilgrimage with all its promise of knowledge, were not the Pyramids first conceived and created in the mind—a mind not unlike your own? Is not the compassionate wisdom of the guru's heart the same flickering flame that is found at the center of all hearts? The hairs on your body are like the trees of a living forest, and the blood that runs through your veins is no different than the rivers and oceans of the Earth. To say that only a distant mountain top is holy and therefore possesses greater access to the secrets of the Universe is to deny the sacredness of your own being, which, though dwelling in the darkest cave, remains forever connected to God. . . . All that you would seek is already within you— waiting to be embraced."

The coldness of passing breezes on my face made me realize tears were falling as I sat in awe. My hand reflexively wiped my cheeks, and I again looked up at the twinkling heavens. Though still fearful, I was stunned by the beauty of what I was hearing.

"Once you honor this natural ability to access the truth, you will derive knowledge from all things, and everyone you meet will be your teacher. You will see sacred Earth wherever you walk, and each day of your life will be a step toward enlightenment—for in truth your pilgrimage began when you were born. . . ."

I had no idea what to do next. Suddenly, I was back to having no real direction for my life; but that didn't seem to be my biggest problem anymore. I now felt the panic of going crazy, yet at the same time I gratefully accepted these words as sanity finally breaking through.

"You do indeed have a destiny to fulfill, but it is only through the inner journey of your Spirit that it will be realized."

Totally humbled and silenced by this marvelous discourse, it was quite some time before I was coherent again. . . .

At last, after a prolonged silence and sensing it was safe, I took a deep breath and slid down off the truck to dig the keys out of my jeans when a somewhat irreverent image fashioned a smile on my face—that of the Lone Ranger serial where, at the end of each episode, the inevitable by-stander says, "Who was that masked man?"

•   •   •

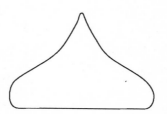

We know who we are by what we do,
And by the reactions of friends and foes,
Though we proudly wear each definition anew,
In truth we lie hidden beneath these clothes.

Chapter Four

The Realm of the Magician

It wasn't long before the continuous whir of the tires faded from my awareness, leaving an expectant silence as I settled back into a monotonous driving rhythm again. Its compelling words still echoing off my thoughts, I tried to form a mental image of whatever was behind this voice, but all I got was conflicting impressions. "Could I summon it whenever I wanted?" I wondered. Even though fearing that I might not have any control over it if it did return, I finally concluded there was only one way to find out. Cautiously I whispered, "Who are you?"

"You wouldn't believe me," came the instant reply. "That's something you best discover on your own."

Although this answer did nothing to assuage the persistent fear that I was becoming delusional, its friendly tone was immediately engaging. "Not that I'm complaining, but why are you just coming into my life now?"

"I'm not."

"You're not coming into my life?" I blurted out in immediate surprise.

"I've been here all along."

Strangely, I exhaled an unexpected sigh of relief before realizing that this brought up a whole new set of questions.

"I've been yelling, jumping up and down, and drawing

pictures for you it seems like forever. . . without overwhelming success, I might add. . . not that I'm complaining."

"What are you talking about? Are you trying to tell me you're some sort of guardian angel or something?"

"Don't be silly. Guardian angels take their jobs much too seriously."

"Don't tell me you're some entity that's trying to take over my body?" I asked that mostly in jest, but it seemed prudent to cover all the bases.

"Hardly. All you have to do is say you don't want me bothering you and I'm gone. . . . For right now, just consider me a friend."

"I've never had a conversation with myself like this before. If you're my 'friend,' what exactly are the other voices I've heard. . . the few other times I've talked to myself?"

"They're the voices of who you think you are."

"How can I be talking to who I think I am?"

"Let me give you an example. When I ask you who you are, what comes to mind?"

A few definitions popped up but I wasn't sure if they were the right answer. . . .

"Yeah, that stuff. Go ahead and say it."

Seeing that it was pointless to stall, I just thought out loud. "I'm a man, I'm a good lover, I'm generous. . . ."

"That's good. Every example that comes to mind when you ask that question is really a self-definition, and each of your self-definitions is capable of speaking to you."

"How can a definition talk?" I was incredulous.

"Picture yourself riding on a bus. Because looking at life through the window of a moving vehicle can be confusing at times, it's helpful to have a tour guide providing information about the scenery. Since you define yourself as a man, it's essential that you have a narration of the scenery from the man's point of view. So, a little image of yourself as a man appears in the front of the bus, picks up the microphone and begins to describe to you the life situations you are currently going through. You also define yourself as a good lover. This creates another little talking image of yourself actively providing some tips, which, to put it in his typical crude vernacular, might help you get lucky at the next stop. The more definitions, the more tour guides."

Somehow the analogy seemed too simplistic, so I just smirked.

"How do you know when it's time for some chocolate ice cream?"

Now we were getting into more familiar territory. "It's always time for chocolate ice cream."

"Okay, how do you know when it's time for making love?"

"That's easy. . . right after the chocolate ice cream."

"It is good to know your priorities, isn't it? But, what I want to know is how do you decide what it is you want to do in any given moment?"

I responded with the obvious. "I guess I look at all the options available and then choose."

"That's what most people think they're doing, however there comes a point when there are so many tour guides in the bus that all the windows become blocked and to know what's going on outside you have to rely completely on their descriptions. Unfortunately, only the guides closest to the microphone get through to you. The rest are sort of lost in the din. Your options are therefore narrowed down to only the loudest voices in your head."

This was interesting, but I wasn't at all sure what it had to do with my current crisis with Dawyn. Absentmindedly, I reached toward the radio with the idea of finding some relaxing background music. . . .

"Do you remember your sixth birthday?"

The question caught me off guard, and I could feel my eyes slowly unfocus as I pensively peered out the dirty windshield into the past. . . . I did remember that day. I awoke in the early morning twilight, immediately frustrated with the unmistakable pungent smell and damp sheets from again failing to wake up when my bladder had obviously signaled "full." My anxiety was further fueled by the acrimonious sounds of my parents arguing in the next room, obviously quarreling over my untrained sphincter muscle. Suddenly, my father burst through the door in deliberate stride. Reflexively, I crouched down, initially anticipating a scolding of some sort, but he didn't even look in my direction. He was through the room in seconds, followed by the sounds of the front door opening and shutting with abrupt anger, and my mother crying in the kitchen. It wasn't until years later that I was able to see that their marriage was in bad shape even without my bed wetting, and the fact that my father chose that day to leave the relationship had nothing to do with a scared six year old boy.

"Do you remember what you thought at that moment?"

I was sure that because I had wet the bed they were angry with each other and with me. What registered was the idea that if I could just do what they wanted, they would love each other again and also love me. . . . I now plainly saw how I had thought love was dependent on my performing in a certain way.

"That perception, that definition of yourself as someone needing to perform to be loved created one of the first tour guides on your bus; and, though not clearly seen over the years, it has been hogging the microphone ever since."

I didn't want to admit it; but, as an awful sadness suddenly descended, I could see I had spent most of my time with Dawyn desperately trying to figure out what I could do to get her to love me again, driven by the unexamined belief that if I could just discover those things she wanted from me and then provide them I would once more have her love. It felt strange and more than a little annoying to be seeing for the first time such an old and dominant pattern of thought in my head.

"Can you also hear what that guide is saying about Dawyn?"

"Oh, shit." Instantly I realized that just as I felt I needed to perform to get her love, I was also expecting her to perform for my love. Among other things, I saw the monument of importance I had placed on how often we made love. It was only when we were "performing" with physical intimacy that I felt her love and could fully show my love.

"Yet you committed to love her unconditionally, regardless of how many times you made love each week."

Every time I had withdrawn my love, every time I had put a condition on it, I had felt a little guilty. Obviously, somewhere inside of me I did know that I wasn't keeping my commitment, but I hadn't seen any other choice.

"That guide from your sixth birthday has learned just what to say over the years to convince you that what it's saying is the only way to go. The newly arrived voice for unconditional love didn't stand a chance."

"How does that happen? There's got to be a way around it."

"Strangely enough, there isn't. This process of creating a set of beliefs and self-definitions that guide you through life is normal and unavoidable, and ultimately even beneficial."

"Beneficial? Of everything you've said, that's the hardest thing yet to believe. And, I don't understand how a process so obviously flawed could be natural and unavoidable."

"From birth, your happiness, indeed your very survival, comes to depend on the establishment of beliefs and definitions that form an identity. You then perceive and experience reality based on this identity."

"Wait a minute. Reality is independent of my identity. I mean a stone wall would still be a wall regardless of my particular beliefs and self-definitions."

"Didn't you just discover that you have lived most of your life with the certainty that love could only be gained or given by performing to expectations?"

"That's different," I said with more hope than conviction.

"Is it? The walls you put up within are no less solid than those you erect outside yourself. . . . You carefully observe and experience life, and then logically form conclusions saying, 'This is who I am,' as you did on your sixth birthday. You have lived your whole life with the firm conviction and unquestioned belief that 'I am someone who must perform to be loved.'"

As I listened, the strange thing was I guess I thought everyone had such a belief.

"You have hundreds, even thousands of such beliefs and definitions, which, along with other illusions acquired mostly from your parents, collectively form your identity. And, in turn, your perception of reality is completely determined in relation to who you think you are."

"What do you mean illusions. I can see how that one definition formed on my sixth birthday was a little off. . . ."

"A little?"

"Okay, it was dumb, but I have also defined myself as a man, for instance, and there's some pretty hard evidence to support that as being real."

"Is that a pun or are you just bragging?"

I laughed, realizing I had become very serious. I sat up to shift my weight and eased off the accelerator to resume a legal speed.

"If you asked ten people to give their definition of a man, you would get ten different answers. Even biologically there is a gray area. The notion of what it means to be a man exists nowhere in the Universe except in the human mind. Therefore, that definition is indeed an illusion based solely on current and collective agreement."

I shook my head in defiance, wanting to win at least one point in this discussion.

"Suppose you let go of your particular definition of being a man, would it change who you are?"

"If I stopped seeing myself as a man?"

"Yeah, would it change who you basically are? In other words, let's say that you are a man—that it is a fact. Does not seeing yourself or defining yourself as a man alter that fact?"

"I guess I am who I am whether I fully see myself that way or not."

"Okay, let's say that you are a man but you define yourself as a boy. Would that change who you really are?"

"No. I'd still be a man, but I probably wouldn't always act like one." I felt I was being led down a garden path, but was confident I could find a way out at any time.

"So, defining yourself as a boy would not change the fact that you are a man, but it would limit your experience and expression of being a man."

"Yeah, I guess so."

"Then consider this. Since no belief about yourself can fully describe the entire miracle of who you are, all self-definitions have the inherent liability of limiting the true experience and expression of yourself, just like the subjective perceptions of your sixth birthday have for your entire life. The sum total of your beliefs have become your identity through which you have defined your entire reality, and because of these beliefs you do not really know who you are."

As might be expected at this point, I became aware of some pretty desperate tour guides screaming wildly into the microphone.

"You have become a master of illusions, a Magician, putting together an identity of subjective beliefs upon which your reality is based and behind which you are concealed, even from yourself."

"Okay, let's say I buy most of that. I still have one little question."

"Just one?"

"You say it's my beliefs that limit me? Well, since I obviously believe myself to be a human being with two legs who can walk and run, this also means I define myself as not being able to fly. Now, if I were able to somehow let go of the belief that I can't fly," I continued while sitting up straight sporting a justifiable grin, "would this mean I could jump off a cliff and soar away like a bird?"

"Because some have done just that in altered states of consciousness and plunged to their death, you already know the answer, don't you? However, I must tell you something. . . . Birds do not fly because they have wings—they have wings because they fly."

I wanted to gloat a little longer over my own salient point but instead pensively repeated the words being said to me as if somehow knowing something important was hidden within them. . . .

"Birds were soaring in Spirit long before their bodies developed the winged ability to ride the wind. Man does fly by taking his machines, some weighing hundreds of tons, into the sky with him. Were man not able to release limiting beliefs about the apparently impossible, he would still be Earth bound. The Spirit's desire always precedes the physical ability."

I looked around the dimly lit cab with tired eyes and realized I had a headache. "Then, what do I know for sure about life and what do I know from just my limiting beliefs?" I wondered to myself while chewing my lower lip, lost in thought. . . . In this aloneness I again felt the inconsolable pain of not having Dawyn's love and the depression of not wanting to live without it. "Where are these thoughts about death coming from?" I asked, really wanting relief more than understanding.

"I know it is hard to believe, but you are in an extraordinarily wonderful place in your life right now."

That was more than hard; it was impossible.

"Your confusion and pain indicate that you have not given up. They are a natural part of your journey and always precede remarkable insights."

I took a deep breath, wanting that to be true. "That's the second time you've mentioned a journey?" I stated quizzically.

"Yes, the Spirit's Journey. There are several specific phases of awareness encountered when traveling the path through the illusions of your identity to who you really are."

"If I'm not who I think I am, then who the hell am I?" Hearing the anger in my own voice brought home how genuinely frustrated I was.

"Who you are can only be experienced."

I wanted a more tangible response than that. "Well, what will I find at the end of this Spirit's Journey?"

"I was afraid you were going to ask that. . . . To tell you the truth, I'm not completely sure. I haven't been all the way to the end, yet, myself."

"What! Then how do you know it's worth the effort?" My tone was challenging but also conveyed my fear of another major disappointment.

"Well, I can assure you that, at the very least, you will find everything your heart currently desires."

"I'll find my destiny? My true destiny?" My eyes grew wide with excited relief as I pictured how happy I'd be if that were really true.

"Yes, your destiny is on this path, waiting for you, just as you have always suspected."

"You're sure. . . and, as part of that destiny, to find that special one meant just for me and experience true love?" This was irresistible, as if holding Aladdin's Lamp.

There was a slight chuckle before my "friend" responded. "Yes, the one you seek and the miraculous experience of true love is there, also."

Now, all I needed to do was locate the fine print in this offer, which I knew would be hidden somewhere. "So, how long does this Spirit's Journey take?" I asked, tempering my enthusiasm with caution.

"Given your current condition. . . I'd say you have about a year left."

Its tone was resolute without any boast. Did it mean it would take someone like me a year to complete such a journey or that I had only a year left period? I wondered if it was just kidding with me again, which immediately returned my skeptical curiosity about this whole phenomenon. "So, all these other voices in my head are merely aspects of my identity?"

"Yes."

"But, you're not."

"I am not part of your identity."

I was totally intrigued by this mystery. "Does everyone have a 'friend' like you?"

"Everyone can connect in their own way with such an internal 'friend,' that is if they allow themselves to let go of those limiting beliefs that prevent such communication. Of course, some cases are much more difficult than others. . . ."

I could hear its words turn to laughter as they faded, and I smiled. Although I wanted to, I wasn't at all sure I really believed this notion about a Spirit's Journey. But, on the other hand, what did I have to lose other than a few more months of an already wasted life. Besides, I could probably proceed on my more logical trek toward enlightenment at the same time. ... "Okay, I'll do it," I ventured impulsively but proudly, and changing the subject. "I'll take this Spirit's Journey. . . ." Again there was laughter, this time much louder and longer. I kept a smile but began to fidget with the steering wheel. "What's so funny?" I finally asked when it seemed I'd be heard.

"I'm sorry. It's just that you already made that choice. . . a very long time ago."

Even if it were true, I didn't think it was **that** funny, but joined in with a nervous little laugh of my own, probably out of politeness. I rolled down the window to let the cold night air swirl around me for awhile and ward off sleep in hopes of continuing a dialogue. But, as I crossed into Colorado, my thoughts involuntarily returned to a beautiful woman in London about to board a jet plane.

•   •   •

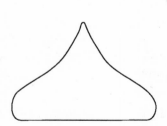

We surround ourselves with all manner of stuff,
Proclaiming, "I am what you see,"
But such assertions are never enough
To silence the dream, "There is more to me."

Chapter Five

The Dream of the Wanderer

With bitter-sweet anticipation, I picked her up at the airport late the next day. She was as lovely and full of life as ever. We quickly shared the highlights of our separate sojourns before I impatiently asked if she'd given any more thought to our relationship. I could see in her eyes that she didn't really want to talk about it. Rationally, I must have known she was concerned about her teenage daughter who was going through a life crisis at the time; but in my way of thinking, all other problems would easily work out if Dawyn would just recommit to the relationship. As I fearfully expected, she felt essentially the same as before she left. I was angry and hurt, and I didn't want to let her off that easily. So, I unleashed the heavy artillery. I produced all our courtship letters in which we had proclaimed our undying love. However, she remained immune to this tactic. Instead, she began calmly and patiently trying to explain her feelings and confusion. I realized I was defeated when she concluded by implying that co-dependency was the major problem in most relationships.

I had no understanding what she was talking about, except that it wasn't what I wanted to hear. I thought briefly about telling her what had happened to me in Boston. That might get to her, but it could also kill any chance of her loving me again. And, what if she didn't care? What if I exposed my vulnerability and she didn't care? Besides, did I really understand that escapade? I was afraid I had lost her, so I went and did the one thing that could guarantee it. And yet, I couldn't have done anything else, in my mind, and survived. No, I decided to give her what she wanted and just let her reap the consequences.

Within a few days I was sitting reflectively in a small apartment of my own overlooking the Flat Irons, a dramatic section of mountains, just west of Boulder and about thirty miles north of Dawyn. I rented it for one month; that would be enough time for Dawyn to come to her senses. Besides, I would need this time to prepare anyway, for any reconciliation would require the exact amount of painful hesitation on my part to induce the obligatory amount of self-recrimination on her part.

As the weeks passed without any contact between us, I realized I might have overestimated her will power. Of course, when anyone asked, I would swear that I had resigned myself to the fact that our relationship would never be the same; but it wasn't what I wanted to believe. However, after two interminable months, I had to admit the truth—I really had lost my divine partner and was never going to achieve the destiny I wanted (and certainly deserved). Alone and lost in my darkened apartment, and with no career, no income, and no interests other than a dying curiosity to know why I had been robbed of happiness, I cried out, "What the hell do I do now?"

"You're doing it, and very well I might add."

I smiled self-consciously, but also in the comfort of hearing that friendly voice again. "Nice to hear from you. . . . Been on vacation?" I obviously wanted to share my bad mood.

"I've been right here, screaming in your deaf ears as usual."

I took a deep breath and casually rubbed my eyes. "I guess I've been pre-occupied."

'That's understandable. A certain amount of grieving is normal for this phase of the journey."

"Sure I'm not heading in the wrong direction?"

"You're doing fine. Your Magician in the first phase of the journey did a real good job of veiling who you are, but there is an aching inside to know the truth that's leading you on to the next phase."

"I don't know if I really believe in this journey stuff. Sometimes I sense there's more to my life than what I've known, but. . . ."

"When you dream, do you not react to your dream as if it were real?"

I nodded my head.

"And, have you ever had a dream that seemed totally real yet some part of you knew you were dreaming? It often happens just before waking up."

"Yeah, I guess so."

"A part of you knows you are dreaming, yet you remain in the dream reacting to the imaginary events as if they were real. Well, in the second phase of the Spirit's Journey, that of the Wanderer, you begin to wake up from the dream-like illusions of your identity."

"How does the Wanderer differ from the Magician?"

"The Wanderer is the Magician who becomes frustrated and disillusioned by following all the voices in his head yet never really attaining happiness or finding fulfillment. Driven by a vague but persistent sense of something more, he wanders through his identity-based reality seeking to discover what is real—searching for himself."

"That has a ring of truth to it, but I'm not really controlled by these voices from my beliefs. I can shut them off fairly easily, like when I want to diet I simply don't pay attention to the voice that wants ice cream."

"Maybe a different example in your life would be more illustrative. You have a belief of yourself as being someone who has a soulmate-type special person who will 'match' you perfectly. . . ."

Something told me I'd be better off sticking to the "ice cream" example.

". . . . The voice of this belief has been a strong one, with specific pictures of what that relationship will look like. When you met Dawyn, this voice told you that your dream was coming true and at first things seemed to match these expectations. But, in time, the relationship stopped fitting your pictures exactly; so, you began to focus exclusively on the gap between what was happening and what you pictured should happen. . . ."

I suddenly wished I had something with which to counter so that my falling in love didn't sound so mechanical.

"The stronger your identity, in other words the stronger the belief that you have a soulmate, the stronger the pictures of what will make you happy. Yours were and are strong, indeed—strong enough to suggest that not attaining such a relationship makes your life not worth living. . . ."

Hearing my grim but dramatic intention presented in this manner definitely reduced its romantic color.

"You have thousands of beliefs that make up your identity, and each belief has attached to it a picture of what needs to occur in your life to make you happy; but life never quite fits these pictures. It is through this process of trying to manipulate what goes on around you to fit your beliefs and pictures of happiness that all your pain and confusion are created."

"Wait a minute. At least some of my pain and confusion have come from outside. What about the Vietnam episode? That was the system and my family doing a real number on me."

"Unfortunately that, too, was a product of your beautifully constructed identity."

Not too terribly thrilled with where this was headed, I briefly wondered if I could get away with taking a snack break.

"You had acquired definitions of yourself as someone who honored your parents and of needing to perform to feel loved. But, over the years, you pulled together some other beliefs that also defined you as someone who was capable, intelligent, and able to march to his own drum. These conflicting beliefs created the unenviable situation that whether you fought the draft or went to Vietnam, you would experience some pain, confusion, and guilt."

"But isn't this process good in a way. I mean this is how someone develops a conscience, isn't it?"

"This is simply the way society passes on its 'shoulds.' And it assumes that your basic nature needs such additional instruction, which is not true. The guilt and depression caused by such conflicting beliefs only present road blocks on the Spirit's Journey and are the basis for all mental illness, not that you have to worry about that." My head was reeling. It seemed too simple. In a way, I didn't want to believe that I was really so uncomplicated. It was implausible that the spectrum of my emotions and behavior were simply a direct result of my conflicting beliefs and my focusing on the "gap" between what I perceived my life to be and what I wanted it to be. I recalled my scholarly apprenticeship in the many established fields of psychology that laboriously try to explain the differences among people. Could it be that this common, though individualistic, process of simply establishing the beliefs of an identity accounted for all the variations of personality?

Struggling, my mind stumbled on the memory of my one exposure to Buckminster Fuller. As a naval officer during World War II and while casually watching the ship's wake from the stern one day, he noticed that literally millions of bubbles were being constantly created in the water by the churning propellers. Having studied engineering, he knew that to design a curved surface like a bubble required using the Greek symbol psi, an infinite number needing to be rounded off at some point and making each calculation an estimate. Going against all his trained logic, he intuited that nature would never use a method of creating bubbles that was so imprecise or complicated. Thus he went about designing a bubble made out of triangles. Not only did this "geodesic dome" prove to be stronger than any conventional type of construction, years later electron microscopes revealed the molecular composition of nature's bubbles to be millions of tiny, straight-edged triangles, giving only the appearance of a continuous curved surface.

I wondered if nature would really use the complicated and imprecise theories suggested by traditional psychology to shape us, or did She employ a simpler, more reliable process as when making bubbles? But, still not wanting to let go of all those psychological tenets so carefully memorized, I was eager to ask more of my "friend" when the phone rang. . . .

•   •   •

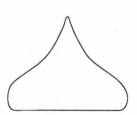

We know not the courage it takes to live
Until all of life seems in vain,
And just at the moment when there's no more to give,
Arises the Warrior to release our pain.

Chapter Six

The Time of the Warrior

I was happily surprised that it was Dawyn calling; but, being half asleep, I asked her to repeat her improbable question. I couldn't have heard her correctly. She told me that she was planning a trip to the West coast in about a week to live with the rest of the One-Earth organization. In a rather casual voice, she wanted to know if I'd like to accompany her with the intention of possibly living together again, but this time in a community setting that supported our expressing love for others, also.

We had seen each other a few times since I had moved out, even spent the night together, but the distance between us had not shortened. The vague and business-like invitation I was hearing on the phone seemed foreign, compared to the former passionate expressions to create with me a full and ever-expanding committed relationship. I suppose there may have been a bit of sadness in her voice about how things had changed, and maybe a tinge of wanting to at least share something pleasant with me. But all I heard was what wasn't there. After all she had put me through, I was amazed at her presumption to even venture such a ludicrous and anemic proposition. And, I was even more bewildered to hear myself, in an equally civil tone, agreeing to go.

We met at the airport on the appointed day. I was glad to see her again, though there was the immediate but contained swell of unresolved feelings within me screaming for attention. It was well passed midnight before our plane landed, and we found ourselves at a friend's house in Palo Alto, together in bed for the first time in months. I never tired of touching Dawyn. She was on the left as usual, my arm cradling her head which rested on my shoulder, her body gently curled into the contour of mine. My right hand was free to silently sift through her soft brown hair and massage her scalp. She loved that and was soon purring. I shifted my position so that I could rub the supple skin of her neck and back, eliciting an occasional sigh. Part of my overwhelming love for her was a great admiration for what she wanted to do in the world. I felt that in my own way, when I gave her pleasure, I was contributing to those noble aspirations and dreams. My hands began to caress her body in ways I knew she liked. I slowly kissed her lips, the side of her neck, her breasts, and all the secret places we had discovered together. I knew by heart every breath she would take, every sigh and moan, every clench of the sheets, and every arch of her back as she floated into ecstasy. . . .

We resumed our snuggling position as her rush of energy slowly subsided. Her thoughts seemed to drift and within a few minutes she was asleep. "She'll want to make love to me in the morning when she's not so tired," I comforted myself with optimistic patience. But, with the sun, she arose quickly without such inclination.

The day promised to be hot and muggy as we drove toward the first of the many scheduled meetings. I finally asked, "Why didn't you make love to me last night or this morning?" I tried to say it with curiosity; however it is possible that a little unintentional, though perfectly justified, resentment seeped into my tone.

She didn't answer right away, maybe distracted with upcoming agendas, or maybe to think of what to say. Then, she quickly countered that she had just wanted to get up and start the day.

To me that meant, of course, that she didn't want to. She always had that right to say no; it wasn't this right that I was questioning, really. I knew not to equate making love with being loved, at least in theory. It was her desires, or lack of, that I wondered about, especially with the stated intention of this trip.

"I also think it's really important that we not be so co-dependent," she concluded with sincerity, but with finality.

There's that word again, or is it two words? Annoyed, I started to ask her what it meant but, thank God, realized that relying on her for the definition of co-dependency would probably be the epitome of what it was. Obviously, our predestined relationship had lost it's Karmic ingredient, even though I was sure we had truly come together with tangible quantities of that divine sweetener. How could this have happened? If a relationship is Karmic, doesn't that mean it will always be Karmic, or is it like chewing gum—sensational in the beginning but bland after a little use? That's what this felt like, a chewed wad of Karmic bubble gum, Dawyn tired of trying to find the lost flavor and me still dreaming of blowing the world's biggest bubble.

At lunch most of the group jumped in a nearby small pool to cool off. I painfully watched her frolic, spontaneously sharing her joy and love with the others. Maybe I was just too sensitive. Maybe she was that joyful with me, too, and I just couldn't see it anymore because it didn't look the way I wanted. I wanted to join them, but I didn't feel they were my friends; they were her friends. My friends would ask her about the commitments she had made. My friends would be able to see my pain, even if I didn't want or know how to express it.

Sad but resolute, I excused myself from the meetings and also from Dawyn's life, returning on the next plane to Boulder. The phone was again ringing as I trudged into my apartment and, with only a minor hesitation to prepare what I would say if it were Dawyn, I answered it. . . .

•   •   •

I had met Jacquelyn several years before. While employed as a Training Manager in an electronics corporation, I contracted with this beautiful, energetic, green-eyed psychologist to conduct some stress management classes for the company. There was a definite attraction between us; but, because she was involved with some guy she reasoned was better husband material than I, we resorted to becoming good friends with a constant flirtatious undercurrent. She was extremely disarming because, although in her thirties, she looked about twenty yet was very competent in her profession, two attributes that complemented each other well in the male-dominated business environment. Unfortunately for her, she had one little peculiarity which, though having become fascinating to me, presented a potential minor drawback for anyone in pursuit of a traditional professional career—she "channeled."

When she first cautiously revealed to me that she was occasionally taken over by entities from other dimensions that spoke through her, I was only mildly intrigued. Up until that point in my life, my only exposure to channeling had come through watching an exposé or two on television about such well-known channels as Ramtha and Mafu (or was that Tofu?). However, unlike these more traditional mediums, most of Jacquelyn's channeling was involuntary. She could be out on a date in a restaurant, blithely chatting away, when all of a sudden her eyes would roll back, her body become rigid, and her hands extended along some imaginary vertical line in front of her with fingers held tensely apart. She would then began speaking in a methodical cadence with a voice at least an octave lower than normal. Most disconcerting of all, however, was the fact that during the "entity's" monologue, she would engage in loud, continuous belching along with assorted bodily contortions to accommodate particularly large eructations. Sometimes she could feel these animated episodes about to commence and prevent them or at least remove herself to a more isolated location before their emergence. Some sites, such as churches, seemed to be especially conducive for facilitating these uncontrollable possessions, which made attending events like weddings and funerals a real adventure. As one might expect, her most proper fiancé, being a traditional Catholic, a West Point graduate, and a typical conservative executive, lived in constant anxiety whenever in public. In any event, my friendship with her had afforded me the opportunity to study this interesting spectacle, which was never really as convincing to me as it was entertaining.

As Jacquelyn returned my "hello" on the phone, I could tell she was in tears. Her engagement was off and her health was deteriorating. I listened to her current travails for quite a while, periodically offering numerous valuable insights. However at the end of our conversation, I was left with only about five minutes to relate the highlights of my current misfortunes, which necessitated my giving the perfunctory impression that I was handling my disastrous life admirably. But because of her considerable training to listen between the lines, she quickly deduced my preoccupations and responded by itemizing the major descriptors of my current situation; I was still confused about my life's purpose, unsuccessful in creating a primary relationship, and depressed to the point of bordering on suicide. She further pointed out that these were common occupational hazards of the typical therapist and that it was obviously time for me to come back and enter the counseling arena again, possibly with her. We ending up laughing like old times, and she said good-bye with inviting words of gratitude. I hadn't really considered returning to California, but Jacquelyn's suggestion that I do so in time to accompany her on a vacation to Maine resurrected some long forgotten fantasies, dormant but obviously not dead, which out of chivalry I felt compelled to at least consider.

Within two weeks I had again sold everything that wouldn't fit in my pickup, which was becoming a rather time-consuming and expensive habit, and had pointed my truck west with only one planned detour between me and a well-deserved repose in New England.

·   ·   ·

Mount Shasta was as beautiful, if not more so, than I had remembered. Exactly one year earlier I had started up the same trail from Bunny Flats; it was good to be back, this time to impress no one. It simply felt appropriate to again do something that signified a transition point in my life. I hoped to locate the ledge where the sacred stones were buried, if I could, and then go on to the summit.

I was taking little gear, only what I would need to get to the top and back in one day. There was a lot less snow pack than the previous trek, which made for more work because the exposed shale and rubble provided extremely poor footing. I headed for what looked like the ridge at which that I had camped, just east of a large outcropping of rock called the Thumb. After six hours of climbing, I was within a hundred feet or so of the shoulder that separated the eastern and southern slopes. The ever changeable landscape took on a familiarity, and I began walking that last bit of distance solemnly. Even though it was unlikely that other hikers had come this way over the last year, I doubted my discarded equipment would still be on the ledge, now just over the approaching rim, because the often inclement weather would have surely claimed it. However, if someone had been drawn there by the bright orange sleeping bag, it was conceivable that they might have found the buried sacred stones. I toyed with the idea of digging them up to make sure they were safe and possibly even keeping one for a souvenir.

As I reached the rim and looked down on the eastern panorama, a shudder went through my body. There was nothing but ice stretching from my feet to the forest many miles below. The glacier had grown measurably and now spilled out over the top of the ridge. Its underside, slowly melted by the sun-heated rocks, had pulled away from the mountain creating an ominous, jagged ravine about two feet wide and sixty feet long. My gaze travelled into this dark, unusual ice-crevasse about twenty-five feet straight down to where the glacier's belly again adhered to the rocky slope. I could see that the ledge where I had placed the sacred stones was no longer there, apparently sheared away and entombed during the winter by the weight of this frozen river. For quite some time I remained transfixed in the presence of such power. . . finally chuckling at myself for even thinking about retrieving one of the sacred icons.

It was another arduous hour of climbing before I was standing alone on the top of the mountain, marveling at the view through clear skies. Relaxing in the sunshine, I took off my hiking boots to sit cross-legged and closed my eyes. I was lost in thought for what seemed like a half hour when suddenly there was a thunderous and unexpected explosion, like the sound of a bomb going off right above my head. My body reflexively jerked and my eyes blinked opened to reveal a dark, billowy fog that had enveloped the entire mountain. I was unable to see more than a few feet in any direction. The explosion had obviously been thunder and, like amorphous dynamite, detonated around me again and again, though I saw no lightning.

The deafening tumult of swirling dark clouds seemed a portentous representation of my life, which felt ever ready to explode. Outwardly, I was looking forward to escaping from my turmoil with Jacquelyn, but underneath I continued in despair. Here I was on some distant mountain top, totally alone, not sure of any aspect of life, and my only comfort some imaginary "friend" that I didn't dare talk about with anyone. Why had this errant life happened to me? Hadn't I tried to do all the right things, gone down all the prescribed paths? Where was that promised person—that love to make life truly worth living? I wanted to believe I was on a Spirit's Journey, but this path had yet to feel too much different than the previous ones. No matter how I tried to rationalize my fortunes, emotionally I remained devastated and never more lost. . . . Later that night camping at the base of the mountain, I fell into an uneasy sleep in which a vivid dream immediately appeared:

"Long ago, from a small village somewhere in Palestine, a young peasant girl, whose name was Sarra, visited the nearby marketplace and, using the few pennies she had saved in her short life, purchased some rare and exquisite apple seeds from the Orient. Her parents and friends shook their heads but said nothing as they had become accustomed to her aloof and unusual ways. Excited to plant these seeds in fertile soil, she hurried off on her own toward the communal orchard she tended quite some distance from the village. So great was her anticipation and desire, she decided this day to take a short cut.

"Between the village and the orchard were large, gently-sloping hills, which, like mammoth fingers, connected her valley with the high mountain range to the east. Her usual path would have taken her around these rocky inclines, but today she reasoned that it would be faster if she traversed over the barren mounds of stone. Being rather frail and diminutive from a sickly childhood, she breathed a sigh of relief upon reaching the top and paused momentarily to enjoy the view. She was hoping to find a trail or path on the other side, but there was none as few people travelled these hills. Feeling her excitement returning, Sarra began an exuberant descent when suddenly her foot slipped on one of the many loose stones, causing her to twist to one side and almost fall. She quickly righted herself and continued on, unaware that one of the precious seeds, so carefully wrapped in a silk cloth at her waist, had jostled free and fallen among the rocks. When the young girl finally reached the fields of the orchard, she lovingly uncovered and planted her treasure in the rich soil, unaware of the one, lost seed on the barren hill above. At the end of five years, all of the trees in the valley were twice Sarra's height and were producing bushels of apples. But, such was not the fate of the one she had dropped.

"The first few months had been very difficult for the forgotten seed. Fortunately, there was enough moisture in the crevice for it to germinate, sending out a lone tendril that patiently burrowed into a granite fissure. With that foothold it was able to send up a small leafy shoot and begin collecting as much sunlight as it could to ward off the cold nights. It grew slowly, paced by the small amount of nutrients it could gather from the unyielding stone and the morning dew. After five years it had only grown to about four feet in height, with just two main branches near the top of its stubby trunk, permanently twisted toward the east by the constant wind that swept the mountain side. And its few dozen leaves, seemingly inadequate to support life, gently caressed but one blossom. . . ."

I awoke excited. I loved parables and to have this one come through me was exhilarating, even if I didn't quite know its meaning. Exhausting my flashlight, I carefully wrote it down and read it several times, polishing as I went and finishing with the self-congratulatory comment, "This is great."

"That was a good one, wasn't it?"

Because I hadn't been listening internally for some time, when I heard its voice I had to smile as if truly greeting an old "friend." "Especially considering I don't usually remember my dreams. . . . Maybe you could give me a little help deciphering it?"

"I can give you a clue."

"Okay." I figured a clue was all I'd need anyway.

"The promise of every apple seed is, of course, to become a healthy tree bearing lots of fruit. Why then would the Universe allow this abandoned seed to be robbed of its promise?"

Having totally forgotten my earlier preoccupation on the mountain, this hardly seemed like a clue, but I assumed a look of contemplation anyway.

"This will probably take you awhile, so why don't we talk later?"

There was an unusual abruptness in its words; but it was just as well, for I was tired from all the writing and wanted to get some sleep before the sun came up. I awoke at first light and listened again for the inner voice but heard nothing. I began looking at its parting question, which I had scribbled down, when suddenly I realized that I had dreamt a second dream...

"Long ago in a small Syrian village, an old Muslim woman, considered to be a wise and spiritual leader to the people of her village, was startled awake by a foreboding dream. From the day of her birth, she had been revered as one with special healing talents; so it was not uncommon for her to have prophetic dreams. But the one on this night seemed to carry a particular portent. In this vision she saw a newborn child struggling for life. Apparently in a town many miles to the west, the child appeared to be extremely sensitive to anyone who came near, somehow being able to sense and absorb their anger or pain. Because the child could not yet talk, its parents could only guess as to why it would eat so little or what caused it to remain in a constant, troubled sleep. The woman was shown that this child only had five more days to live unless healed with a blessing from someone who had lived a similar experience and could therefore fill the child with the strength of a knowing compassion. There was no question in the woman's mind as to why this vision had come to her.

"She quickly arose and began collecting some food and water to put in her shoulder sack. Neighbors heard the commotion and were greatly alarmed at her plans. 'You are not that strong, and no child is worth risking your life,' they argued. 'Besides, there are many here that need your gifts and guidance.' She could not disagree with them about the danger, for it did seem like a long and arduous journey to travel alone; yet there was no one to go with her because all the men were in the fields with the harvest and the other women had children to care for. She patiently listened to their protests, but there stirred no hesitation within her heart. One of the things she had learned throughout her life was to follow her intuition, no matter what it required. In doing so she had witnessed countless miracles and had often experienced herself being used as an instrument of healing by a force beyond her comprehension. Having no choice, she left at dawn with one goat skin of water, a loaf of bread, and some cheese, which was all her slight frame could carry.

"To get to the town shown to her, she travelled steadily west into the mountains. It was the beginning of the third day, well into the high country, when she consumed the last of the food and finished the water. By noon the sun was desperately hot, preventing her from walking as fast as she had hoped. Later, as she said her evening prayers in the cold desert air, her thoughts quickly turned away from her own growing shivers of hunger and thirst to the torment of a distant child.

"The next day was equally hot, and there were no more trails to follow as the mountains had become steep ravines of barren rocks and shale. But it was too late to turn back. She painstakingly made her way along the loose and unforgiving ledges in a general westerly direction. By late afternoon she was completely exhausted; and, as another small rock gave way under her foot, she fell to her knees again, this time unable to move any further. Tears, collecting the clinging dust, began to streak down her face. She was weeping, not for herself for her life had been full and much blessed, but for the confused and withering child, whom the old woman now believed would never receive the needed blessing.

"Lying motionless in defeat, she thought she heard a noise, a noise that couldn't possibly be. It was the sound of wind rustling through leaves. She wondered if this was what it was like to be on the verge of death. But, then she heard it again. Wearily, she raised her head and squinted into the setting but still bright sun. She could not believe her eyes. There, about forty feet away, jutting out impossibly from a small crevice, was the miraculous sight of a small, odd shaped, and very old tree.

"She gathered enough strength to stumble over to it and let her body crumple to the ground beneath its few branches, which had all grown twisted to one side. She leaned back against its gnarled but sturdy trunk, positioned herself in the small patch of shade from its few leaves and gratefully fell asleep. Several hours later she awoke to the dim light of the stars and again smiled in amazement and gratitude for her new friend. She reached up to gratefully caress the leaves only to be further surprised by the touch of something firm. She gently pulled, and it released into her palm. Although it was small and pitted, she could not remember ever having eaten an apple that tasted as sweet.

"With the morning sun she could see the valley stretched out in front of her. The landscape looked vaguely familiar, reminding her of where she had spent her childhood tending orchards. Pausing briefly one last time to give thanks and marvel at the strange, weathered tree, she continued on her mission refreshed. By the evening of that, the fifth day, she had reached her destination, the town of Bethlehem, and had found the child, Jesus, upon whom she bestowed her humble blessing."

As I finished writing I set my pen down softly on the ground and stared off through the trees at the sloping foothills in the distance. These dreams were far beyond what I believed to be my creative ability, and I was filled with cautious ebullience.

"Who is to say what the promise or destiny of one's life is?"

I remained motionless as the gentle voice of my "friend" again gathered inside me.

"If the lost seed had felt robbed of its chance at happiness, it would simply have given up and died. It would never have experienced the destiny of nourishing the tired traveller and ultimately becoming part of a needed blessing conferred upon the child."

I lifted my head with the emerging realization that my current funk was again caused by focusing on what I felt I didn't have, thus blinding myself to the things I did have. Although it made no sense, I suddenly felt very powerful.

"Everything else in nature, when handed the miraculous gift of life, lives it to the fullest, regardless of circumstance. The perception of being robbed of a rightful destiny only exists in the mind of man."

A shiver ran up my spine; and I closed my eyes in feigned disgust, "Why do I get caught up in this depression?"

"Even those that find themselves planted near the orchard wish they had been placed in the more fertile soil near the well. Those near the well lament their enviable position because they are expected to bear more fruit. Everyone tends to see their destiny as something other than what they are and what they have."

"But wanting what you don't have is what goals and desires are all about?"

"You've had many desires and set lots of goals in your life. Have they led to your destiny?"

I acknowledged that inarguable point in silence, but concluded on a note of appreciation for the vivid stories. "Thank you."

"There is another to thank for these dreams, not I."

I laughed, at first, thinking that was a joke; but, as the silence continued, I became frightened that possibly another voice was going to start talking to me.

"You can actually thank yourself, a very special aspect of yourself."

"What do you mean?" I cautiously asked while checking to see if I felt anything unusual going on in my body.

"As the Wanderer, you encounter the confusion and pain of your identity-based reality not being able to fulfill you. You feel the fears of not knowing what lies beyond. And, just when you feel defeated by this torment, there arises within you the courage and strength of the Warrior."

I smiled with the image of myself as a proud Indian brave. "So, it is the Warrior in me that is now awakening. . . that brought me these dreams?"

"No."

"But you just said. . . ."

"It is you that is now awakening to your Warrior."

I paused to be sure of the distinction. "You mean he's always been here? Why haven't I seen him before now?"

"It was your Warrior who invited the deer into your Sierra camp long ago, and the one who recently choreographed your dance with the Buffalo. It was he who led you up Mount Shasta and stayed with you through the snow storm. It was also his courage you called upon to give up everything when you chose a life with Dawyn."

I felt strangely comforted. "Why am I just now becoming aware of this guy?"

"Because you are surrendering to the fact that you cannot 'figure' a way out of your current pain; you are surrendering to life, even if it means living your worst fears. It is only at such a point as this that the strength and courage of the Warrior within can truly arise."

I could think of nothing more to say and just sat there with an unexpected sense of confidence. A little later, as I fixed a rather simple breakfast of granola and fruit, I experienced an optimism all but forgotten. With the emergence of this Warrior and its uncommon strength, I now felt I could move very fast along this Spirit's Journey; although I wasn't at all sure in which direction that was. Breaking camp quickly and with ease, but feeling more at home with nature than I ever had before, I took a few hours to hike around the woods before acknowledging that my growing urge to dive head first into the resurrected fantasy with Jacquelyn was obviously the next step toward my fated appointment with destiny.

•   •   •

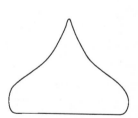

Karma is shared in a familiar sweet smile,
And in the bitter herb of an angry deed,
As the fragrant aroma of all we beguile,
And the unyielding burden of all we need.

Chapter Seven

The Taste of Karma

The next day my overloaded pickup happily rolled to a stop in front of my mother's two-story, stucco house in San Francisco. She was glad to see me even though I was staying just a day or two to unpack and store my things in her basement. Our relationship was really quite good at this point. It had taken me forty years, but I finally accepted the fact that she disapproved of everything I was doing and was disappointed by everything I wasn't doing; a perspective she felt compelled to take as a good mother.

Our most volatile clash had come long ago during the Vietnam era. She was vehemently against my "dodging" the draft, feeling that it was my patriotic duty to go and quite assured in her own mind that her God would protect me. She was equally adamant that my psychology curriculum in college was evil and that I could learn everything I needed to know merely by studying the religious books of her church. So, naturally, she actively condemned anything else that occupied my time like smoking marijuana and engaging in pre-marital sex, although she did allow for kissing but only if engaged. It was during this period that she "just happened" to meet a woman leaving my apartment early one morning. True to form, my mother quickly reduced her to tears with a well-planned tirade about immorality. Exiting a few seconds behind my co-conspirator, I caught only the last few sentences of my mother's captious performance; but, comparing it to other harangues to which I'd been privileged, I'd say it measured only a 7.2 by Olympic standards. However, my demure but startled first wife-to-be, not as familiar with the finesse required for a really good chastisement, gave it a perfect 10. Exercising all my incipient counseling skills, I easily matched my mother's misguided eloquence with an infantile exhibition of my own, which ended with the classic declaration that I no longer had a mother.

For the next two years I had no contact with her, which was probably a mutual relief. I grew a beard during that long hiatus and ended the stand-off by ringing her doorbell unannounced a few days before Christmas. She was in mid-sentence of asking this strange, hairy person what he was selling before realizing that her son awkwardly stood before her. With watering eyes, she impulsively reached out to hug me, a gesture of affection in which she had not indulged since I was thirteen years old. Evidently, this abstinence was a consequence of the values she had adopted from her parents or some well-meaning friend offering advice to a nervous, single mother on how to raise two sons alone.

In the years that followed she was able to occasionally push through her self-consciousness and hug me, but only after adequate periods apart or on holidays. Time had allowed her heart more expression and, except for a few comments under her breath from time to time, she really didn't confront the differences in our values anymore. We just enjoyed our love for one another, such as it was, and avoided words of real personal expression.

•   •   •

Jacquelyn was also glad to see me; and, I had to admit, it felt very good to hold a woman in my arms who wanted to be there. She was free, or so she thought, of her previous relationship and was eager to acknowledge the unexplored chemistry between us, finally verbalizing some of the fantasies she, too, had long suppressed under that very professional veneer. However, to ensure our success in any such fated endeavor, I felt it important to learn everything I could about Karma and its effect on relationships. So, in the few days before we left to spend most of August and part of September at her parents' cabin on Lake Winnipesakee in New England, I read every book I could find on the subject I discovered that the Law of Karma is not so much a law as it is a theory; and, as such, lends itself to being interpreted in a variety of ways, which keeps it shrouded in unresolved controversy.

"For every action there is an equal and opposite (opposing) reaction." This is considered a Law of Motion attributable to Sir Isaac Newton that describes the conservation of energy in the Universe. Karma is generally regarded as the metaphysical equivalent of this law. Essentially it's saying that all the energy it takes to create an action will be accounted for in an associated (opposite) reaction. For instance, jumping into a swimming pool is an action. The water's reaction to that action is to form several circular waves that travel outward from the point of entry. All the energy of jumping into the pool is transferred to the motion of the waves (except for a small amount lost to friction).

Karmicly relating this to life, all of my actions fell into two main categories. First there were the things I did that could be considered good, done consciously, unselfishly, and for the unification of mankind. Then there were the things I did that were hurtful, done non-consciously and selfishly, which tended to separate people. As with jumping into water, my conscious actions created good waves of Karma, and my unconscious actions created bad waves of Karma. These waves would eventually return to wash over me, letting me experience the same effect they were having on others. Good Karma I welcomed, but bad Karma could cause me all sorts of grief, especially when I didn't realize or accept that I had created it.

These theories also endorsed reincarnation, insisting that I had brought previous Karma with me into this life. Therefore, the purpose of this life was to "clean up" all the bad Karma from past lives, along with any current acts of selfishness, and in so doing get off the "wheel of life" by ascending into nirvana (heaven). All Karmic relationships originated somewhere in these past lives where such agreements were made, either consciously or unconsciously, to re-connect in some future life in order to help each other in this noble process. But, I wondered, what one does when a karmicly designed (soulmate) relationship just peters out? The answer I uncovered was not reassuring.

Evidently, if Dawyn and I recognized we had such a relationship, made vows to create a loving life together, and then one of us withdrew from the relationship (creating pain and havoc with the other's life), then that was our Karmic agreement. This meant that regardless of what happened in a Karmic relationship either person could excuse it by simply saying, "Well, this must be what we agreed to do way back in Atlantis." Maybe it was because my life was in havoc rather than Dawyn's, but I didn't particularly like this "safety valve" clause. Not only that, but if Dawyn was creating some bad Karma by dumping on me, I wasn't clear if I'd have to wait until another lifetime before being able to return to her that negative wave of energy (for her own benefit of course)?

Finally, in looking at my potential "bad Karma" in just this life, I arrived at five or six events that probably had initiated waves with negative energy needing to be cleaned up before they returned to wash over me. Estimating that I've had maybe a thousand previous lives, each averaging six negative situations needing immediate attention, it meant that I had roughly six thousand bad Karmic swells headed my way. (Metaphysically, this is known as "surf's up!") "Maybe it was time to check in with my "friend?" I cautiously concluded while pushing the pile of reference books aside and walking out into the backyard sunshine for some much welcomed fresh air.

"Of course Karma exists, but what is it you really want to know?"

"Is there such a thing as a Karmic relationship?"

"Sure.""Alright," I sighed plopping down on the semi-damp grass to receive the expected information like a sponge but heard only the chattering of two sparrows in a plastic bird bath about twenty feet away. "That's it. . . . 'sure?'"

"Well, the first thing you need to know is that the term 'Karmic relationship' is redundant. . . . All relationships are Karmic."

I hadn't read this anywhere. "Even someone I might pass on the beach without saying a word? That's a Karmic relationship?"

"A Karmic relationship is simply one that fulfills its potential to help you become conscious. Dawyn affords you a great opportunity to learn many lessons so you conclude with certainty it's Karmic. Who's to say that the person you pass on the beach, by casually ignoring you, couldn't provide you with an insight, even though slight, that eventually changes your life? Is that any less Karmic?"

I felt myself getting a little tense, which had become normal at the beginning of these dialogues. "You're not going to tell me that my connection with Dawyn wasn't special?"

"Everyone helps each other, whether consciously or unconsciously, in the struggle to learn their lessons. To say that some relationships are Karmic and others are not is to ignore the inherent illuminating potential of all relationships."

"But, what about soulmates? I was sure Dawyn was that special person for me, I mean ten times more sure than all the other women in my life."

"Knowing that you have a predestined soulmate somewhere is a romantic and comforting thought, but it is also a life-consuming preoccupation. You and I would have had this conversation twenty years ago if you hadn't so tenaciously clung to this belief."

"I don't think I want to hear this. . . . You mean there's no such thing as soulmates?"

"Are you asking if there is one specific person fated to be your partner in life and make all your dreams come true?"

"Yeah," I said closing my eyes and squinting as if waiting for a firecracker to go off.

"No."

I took a breath and sat up straight, prepared to argue.

"But, there are soulmate relationships," it continued before I could begin my assault.

"But, you just said. . . ."

"I said there is no one person designated to be your soulmate. Soulmate-type relationships are by choice. . . ."

This idea had possibilities of opening up whole new vistas, though I remained dubious.

"I bet I can describe how you picture your special relationship."

I thought about changing the subject, but I didn't think I could get away with it.

"You see this relationship as lasting for the rest of your life with the two of you living together as a couple, totally and naturally satisfied by each other. You see her as a beautiful fountain of admiration for you, enabling you to find satisfaction and fulfillment in all the other areas of your life. . . ."

"Okay. . . okay."

"Consequently, you could never enjoy the actual relationships you had because you automatically focused on what wasn't matching your pictures of what it should be. . . . As if you really knew what a soulmate relationship was, anyway!"

"Wait a minute! When I'm being drawn into a relationship with the intensity I felt toward Dawyn, there's gonna be a part of me that knows what it should look like, even if just generally." Ah, my passion and logic had finally found each other.

"There is a part of you that knows, but that knowledge is not to be found in the beliefs and pictures of your identity."

"Then, you're saying that Dawyn and I could still be soulmates. . . and I just may not see it clearly?"

"If you two have chosen to be soulmates, then undoubtedly what you are going through is part of such a relationship."

But, how can that be when it's over, fini, kaput. There is no relationship."

You can choose to have one, but you cannot control exactly what that soulmate relationship will look like."

I shook my head and conveniently denied that Dawyn and I were soulmates, and possibly never had been; therefore none of this applied anymore. It was my "friend's" other point that now intrigued me. "Such special relationships are by choice, eh?"

•   •   •

We arrived at the airport about an hour early, time that Jacquelyn used to shop the over-priced boutiques. She had decided to avoid if possible the stressful exercises of channeling entities from other dimensions while on vacation in an effort to improve her poor health of late. However, just to be prepared, I used my pre-boarding time to quickly review in my mind what I had learned from a few recent encounters with that esoteric practice.

Having attended a Whole Life Expo, I had the front row seat opportunity to carefully evaluate the entire performance of Lazaris (or Jack Percell as he is known to the IRS). There was part of me that wanted to believe that the friendly, Scottish brogue coming from this rather diminutive but animated gentleman did indeed originate from a being of higher intelligence in another galaxy. However, I had a healthy off-setting skepticism that quickly calculated the enormous amount of money being collected by Mister Percell for his audio cassettes, video tapes, and personal appearances. I couldn't help considering the temptation for a good actor to perpetrate the unthinkable act of faking the entire thing to take advantage of the many people who want to find the truth through others; or that possibly he had just found a socially acceptable, not to mention lucrative, way of hiding a multiple personality disorder.

Not wanting to base such conclusions on a sample of one, I soon, thereafter, attended a dolphin channeling seminar. This leader's message, while in trance, was essentially the same as the other more conventional entities typically channeled, but her method was definitely unique. She laid down on the floor, remaining quiet for a few minutes while the inter-species connection was made. Then, taking a deep breath, she abruptly arched her back, bringing her forehead and knees toward each other, only to relax again into a prone position while conveying a few words of the message with her exhale. It required several of these undulating motions to recite even a short sentence. She explained this unusual occupational hazard as the way her body reacted to dolphin energy, and I suppose in a very rough fashion it did resemble the swimming motion of our aquatic cousins. However, once again, I couldn't dismiss the irreverent thought that, if I were one of ten hot dog vendors on the same beach, it might occur to me to provide some entertainment at my booth.

On another occasion, I participated in a week-long seminar with Ken Carey, channeling author of *Starseed: The Third Millennium,* at his farm outside of St. Louis, which proved to be a more believable experience. Although I did not see or hear the beings who evidently dictate information to Ken and his wife, Sherry, I did appreciate and accept on an intuitive level his explanation of how channeling occurs for him. He drew a circle in the center of our group, and then turned that circle into a star figure by drawing pie-shaped points stretching from each of the fourteen or so people to the central disc. According to Ken, when channeling in a meditative state, he allows his consciousness to travel (melt) down his particular star point into the center and then, still connected to his origin, out to any other aspect of that star. In this way he can merge with another to communicate but does not lose himself in the process.

Overall, my attitude toward channeling boiled down to wanting to hear a channel tell me something that was specific and indisputably true, something that could only come from someone who was communicating with the "beyond," whatever that might be. I guess I thought I'd know it when I heard it. Until then, I'd let my skepticism remain.

Fortified from these past experiences, I boarded the plane with Jacquelyn, confident that I could handle any uninvited entities and looking forward to evaluating Jacquelyn as a soulmate. All went well until that afternoon. We were on the Massachusetts Turnpike in a rented Ford. Jacquelyn's body became rigid with her eyes held tightly closed as she let out a slow, painful unearthly growl, just one of the various unique signals she used to indicate the presence of a foreign entity in her body. Fortunately, I had chosen to drive; and, since traffic was light, I was able to give her my conscientious, though somewhat intermittent, attention.

Having witnessed these "afflictions" three times before, I expected the usual deep, methodical voice generated by what she had described on earlier occasions as a powerful male energy that invaded her. From these previous possessions, I had ascertained that this entity was mostly concerned with chastising Jacquelyn for not following its persistent instructions to take better care of herself and to lead a more purposeful life. Since this was not a conflict of interest with my intentions, I tacitly encouraged his presence and usually had a few questions for the ready. However, this time as she began talking, her voice was of normal tone and feminine gender but with a quaint and hitherto unheard Welch accent. Intrigued, I began spontaneously asking questions as if I were a seasoned tabloid interviewer. It turned out that "Myra" was a saucy tart from eighteenth century England with a great sense of humor and a decidedly open mind, obviously ahead of her time. She indicated that I, in one of my past lives, was one of her "regulars" and someone she liked very much. I took this unlikely and unsolicited channeling as a welcomed omen that our current platonic relationship had a good chance of changing by the time Labor Day rolled around.

The picturesque cabin, right on the lake with the famous New England maple trees all around, was just perfect for two people with unexplored desires. Unfortunately, Jacquelyn's parents had also planned their entire month's vacation there and, arriving a couple days ahead of us, laid claim to the only bedroom, setting up a situation where any "guests" would have to sleep on individual cots in the semi-private living room. Her parent's Midwest values notwithstanding, Jacquelyn and I decided to erect a large canvas tent twenty yards from the cabin. This activity was not met with a great deal of enthusiasm; but, since we were consenting adults and weren't "doing it" under their roof, nothing was overtly said.

One afternoon when retiring to our quaint quarters to take a "nap" with Jacquelyn, I had my first real conflict with her primary, male entity. She and I had started to become amorous, an activity I was pleased to see increased her vitality and overall health, when she began to belch abruptly. I sat up with the dreadful thought that possibly erotic stimulation encouraged these unnatural visitations; and I wasn't at all sure how to go about correcting such a scheduling conflict, should it prove to be true. This particular adjustment process as the entity descended into her body was especially difficult for Jacquelyn. It was also evidently painful for the entity as well for it began an unearthly howl, using Jacquelyn's lungs of course, that lasted for several minutes and was undoubtedly heard by her parents and most of the inhabitants in the western part of Maine. Since we were supposedly taking a nap, any bystander's logical assumption would have been that this piercing squeal was probably an impassioned result of a sexually voracious appetite. Jacquelyn, being in a trance, wasn't sharing any of my concern as to whether her parents would ever speak to us again and only got embarrassed later (sans entity) when I drew her a detailed verbal picture.

Finally, summoning the courage to return to the cabin, I decided it was better to volunteer what had actually produced the unholy noise, even though her parents might be less accepting of its metaphysical origins than what I'm sure they had already concluded. It turned out they were much more civilized than I suspected, and the entire vacation was a joy. In addition, the entity proved to be an extremely reasonable chap, and much to my delight I discovered that, when making love, I was the only one occupying Jacquelyn's attention and anatomy.

•   •   •

It was clear to me now: I would choose Jacquelyn to be my soulmate. Being a psychologist, she could help me under-stand and translate my feelings of love and, possibly with more practice, she could also provide assistance to me in the spiritual realm through her channeling. We didn't love each other, at least not with the intensity I had known with Dawyn, but surely that would come as we continued on the soulmate's path. Upon arriving back in the Bay Area, we began living together. It took all of about two months before we were living separately again. Taken on face value, this was not an encouraging turn of events. However, trying to be optimistic, I noticed that half of the time we were together things were pretty good. This was certainly a better percentage than any of my previous relationships.

When we had first set up house, I, of course, concentrated on the importance of my writings to document what I was learning along this Spirit's Journey. Discovering truths about myself and the Universe was very exciting. Naturally, whenever Jacquelyn had a problem or discomfort in her life, as her committed partner I would dutifully apply my precepts, share my analysis, and prescribe a remedy. Although never as excited with this compelling process as I, Jacquelyn, I concluded, was just someone probably a little shy about expressing gratitude for such devoted support. However, by the start of our second month, I detected a slight but distinct streak of hostility arising in her whenever I began to fulfill my mentoring responsibilities. Her reluctance to accept my insights about her problems did little to fuel the progress of my thesis; and, gauging by her renewed interest in other men, it ultimately became apparent to us both that this may not be a match made in heaven.

I became more than just a little embarrassed and depressed over this failure, avoiding any meaningful internal dialogue with my "friend" until I could at least try to temper my justified resentment for the relationship not working. . . . "I thought you said soulmate relationships are by choice!'

"I did."

"Well, I chose Jacquelyn, but it obviously didn't work out. So, do you have another theory?"

"Just as you have the sovereign right to choose anyone you want to be your soulmate relationship, Jacquelyn has that right, too. . . . Let me give you a little hint—next time choose someone who also chooses you."

Why did that seem so painfully logical now? "But I thought she had chosen me."

"You guys decided to live together while you were at the lake on vacation, right?"

"Yeah."

"And during that month you were sailing, hiking, eating chocolate ice cream, and making love, right?"

"Well, yeah."

"So you come back, set up house with her, and then you put your warrior-like efforts back into your personal quest for truth, right?"

"Yeah, but it was for her benefit, too. Any insight I had or truth I discovered I made available to her."

"First of all do you think Jacquelyn is any less capable than you to discover her own truths?"

"Well, no. . . but as her partner how can I not want to help her?"

"How do you get your insights and truths?"

"I guess by doing things like living with Jacquelyn and then looking at what comes up in me as a result."

"Exactly—by doing. People learn which insights are valid only through their own experiences. In fact, if someone told you they had discovered a truth that would fit your life, you'd become very suspicious, especially if that person was adamant. You did not allow Jacquelyn the privilege of discovering her own truths."

Its tone was unequivocal, and I became somewhat reticent. "You're being pretty rough about this, aren't you?"

"I'm being helpful—just as you were with Jacquelyn and with Dawyn. . . . That's what it feels like when someone cares more for a belief than people."

I felt a little scolded but also had the feeling it was at least partially deserved. . . .

"Besides, you really can't blame Jacquelyn."

"Well, a little. She could have tried a little harder."

"The only thing more frustrating than striving to be perfect is having a relationship with someone who thinks he is. . . . Who wants to live with a priest?"

"Priest?"

"You might go and visit one on Sundays for an hour or so, but nobody's going to permanently set up house with one!"

"What are you talking about?"

"That's what someone who tries to convert others is called. But, you'll learn more about that in future phases of the journey."

"Future phases? I thought once I got the Warrior's courage to go through all this stuff I was home free."

"The phase of the Warrior means you're about half-way."

"Half-way!?"

"Actually, a little less than half-way."

I was taken back, having thought it was going to be mostly clear sailing after the Warrior. I wasn't sure what to expect now, but at least it meant that I was still on the right track. Obviously, I was in the process of gathering valuable knowledge that would be of great benefit to the masses when my book was published. "This goal, then, would be the ardent focus of my attention from now on," I vowed with a deep breath. I would complete and document this Spirit's Journey, realizing now that this would lead to the destiny of my dreams. Re-dedicated, I switched on the computer and began collecting the scattered notes and jotted insights atop my desk when the ever fateful phone, right on cue, intervened. . . .

•　　　•　　　•

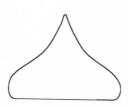

The risks in love, whether stated or unspoken,
Are best not chanced by those too frail,
For all fears are realized and all trusts broken,
When receiving the precious gift of betrayal

Chapter Eight

The Gift of Betrayal

Cheerfully greeting me with forced enthusiasm and a purpose-ful tone was a One-Earth office worker wanting to inform me of all the up-coming activities being planned by that peace organization. I realized instantly she must be a new volunteer as Dawyn and I hadn't spoken in quite some time and most of the others in the "family" were at best indifferent to my active participation in their programs. Rather than trying to explain the long, tragic story, which would have taken much more time than I wanted to give and probably would have inflicted some embarrassment on this naive young lady, I merely listened patiently for the three or four minutes it took her to recite the familiar calendar of events. However, when she finished, there was an unexpected pause. I had thought she would immediately ask me if I were interested in participating or contributing in some way but, instead, her voice trailed off nervously, conveying an air of desperation.

"You used to work here, didn't you?" She tentatively began anew.

"Yes, I did." I sat up a little straighter in the squeaky, oak chair, realizing with pride that my reputation must be greater than I had previously thought.

"You and Dawyn were dating for awhile?"

By that question it was obvious she knew exactly who she was calling. "Well, that's putting it mildly; but yes, we did."

"Can I ask you a question? I need some advice because I don't know what's going on here."

Something told me I should beg off at this point; but, like the proverbial cat, curiosity drove me on. "Sure," I said quickly so as to not reveal my apprehension.

"I suppose you know, but Dawyn is dating my husband and. . . ."

No, I hadn't known, and as soon as she said it I wished I didn't know. My stomach churned. Why was this woman calling me? What could I do about it anyway? I didn't have any influence over Dawyn; and besides, I already didn't even like this woman's husband, whoever he was. I returned to a slouching posture, still holding the phone, and said nothing.

". . . . he's going to leave me and move in with her. . . and I just don't understand what's going on. Can you tell me about her?"

Oh, boy, could I tell you about her. "He's moving in with her?" Now, there was a sage response!

"Well, he actually moved out of our house this morning. . . . I just want to know if you experienced this with her, or if you can give me any advice?"

Me, who until recently knew the number of the Suicide Prevention hotline by heart, was being asked advice on how to save a relationship that's being broken up by the woman who triggered my worst ever depression. The irony, the humor of this situation! The Universe was going beyond the call of duty in orchestrating this one. I was in awe. . . . "How long has it been going on?" I was asking questions now, not so much for curiosity's sake, although I did want to know when this sordid liaison began, but to try and think of something appropriate to say. What could I possibly tell this lady?

"Maybe a month of so. . . ."

I knew it. She couldn't wait to get me out of the picture.

". . . . right after my husband and I volunteered to do some work for the organization. I have to say that we had been having some problems before Dawyn came along, but everything fell apart after that. She was up front about it. They both came and told me they were interested in each other and asked me if it was okay. I said it was. . . because. . . you know, I want to support him in what he wants to do. . . . But, I just don't understand what's really going on."

I could have told her that One-Earth believes a collapse of all the old, social "models" is coming and that people need to develop a new "paradigm" for relationships. I could have tried to explain how everyone in that organization was actively struggling to discover what these new ways of loving each other will look like. But, somehow that all seemed just too abstract. (It's just as well I didn't get into a long discourse because later I would learn that both she and her husband had been experimenting with "open marriage" before Dawyn came along, and that her current panic was the result of a latent anxiety reaction to that mutual decision.)

"Well. . . ." Of course saying "well" wasn't really what I wanted to do either because it committed me. Something perceptive is always expected after such an opening. Suddenly I heard from my inner "friend."

"He's actually given her a gift." The voice was so loud that I froze, wondering if by some chance she heard it, too, as the silence on the other end of the phone just continued.

It became obvious that she hadn't when she finally said, "I suppose I shouldn't have called you. I don't know what you can. . . ."

"He's actually given you a gift." Now, why did I repeat that out loud? She was certain to want an explanation. I think she did respond with something at that point, probably asking what I meant; however I was too busy praying frantically and listening intently for further instructions. . . . "He's given you the gift of betrayal," I continued, this time in my own words, although I knew the thoughts were still attributable to my "friend." I was also thinking to myself that this better be good. ". . . . because when someone you love betrays you, you have the opportunity to experience the true depth and quality of your own love." Not bad, I thought; and this was obviously having some impact on her as again there was silence. . . . "We say we want to be able to love without conditions. Well, a betrayal is the chance to experience the depth of our own hearts. It's the ultimate test of love."

As I listened to myself, I knew what I was saying was true. Somewhere inside of me I had known that there were probably many reasons Dawyn and I had done our dance, though this particular benefit of my feeling betrayed had never before appeared so clear.

". . . . In addition the gift of betrayal lets us go through a fear that can be released in no other way. When needing to love someone, there is a natural fear of losing that person. A fear that life would somehow be less, that we could never be as happy without that relationship. There is, possibly, no way to release this fear and its control over us other than experiencing a betrayal and having that relationship as we picture it end. When betrayed, we have the opportunity to experience that our happiness is not dependent on anyone else and that our own strength and courage will see us through any situation."

"That's an interesting way to look at it. . . ." She said cautiously.

Apparently, she wasn't ready to buy it; and emotionally neither was I. No matter what I might be learning because of my crushed relationship, I was still disbelieving it had to be that way, still not accepting that Dawyn and I couldn't learn what we needed to learn while being together.

"I wouldn't worry too much, though," I continued, unable to resist. "They'll split up in about three months. That's Dawyn's pattern." I'm not sure whether this final piece of wisdom came from my "friend" or not. It got a little fuzzy at that point and just possibly this addendum was more of a wish than a prediction.

I knew the conversation initiated by this distraught, faceless stranger was meant for me as well. I had lost Dawyn and, so far, had survived much longer than expected. I could not have experienced the extent of my own strength in any other way. Additionally, I had promised to love Dawyn unconditionally, regardless of whether she loved me or not. Was my heart strong enough, deep enough, to contain love for someone who had betrayed me? It had been easy to pledge my love to her when she was pledging her's in return. Though maybe not her conscious intent, Dawyn had given me the gift of these experiences. It was time to unwrap that gift and see the full character of my love. Could I forgive her?

Intellectually I could. I could even say it out-loud. But, it was the emotional forgiveness that resisted. This was no ordinary anger; it felt a part of my body, like it had a right to be there and a necessary function to perform. To get past this, if even possible, was going to take something extraordinary.

•   •   •

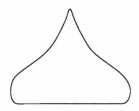

"To err is human, to forgive divine,"
These wise words are the accepted trend,
But, in truth such an act is not so kind,
Because to forgive, we must first condemn.

Chapter Nine

The Fallacy of Forgiveness

I had never done a "sweat lodge" before, and to say that I was less than enthusiastic about such an experience would be exaggerating. However, when a friend of mine insisted on giving me a detailed description of this upcoming ancient American Indian ritual designed to remove stubborn emotional blocks, I somehow knew it wasn't a coincidence. The event was being conducted at Harbon Hot Springs near Calaveras Creek, a picturesque spot at about the four-thousand-foot level on the northeast edges of California's Coastal Range and, according to legend, was the very spot actually used by the native Indians for such ceremonies. First, a round pit was dug about two feet deep and four feet in diameter. The frame for the lodge was constructed over the pit by planting tall green branches every couple of feet in a large circle around the pit and then bending them toward the center to tie where they met, forming a somewhat round structure about four feet high and twelve feet across. Traditionally, large leather hides, which progress had replaced with thick, dark canvas tarps, were then draped on top making the hollow mound almost air tight.

About twenty-two of us gathered at three in the morning with the organizer, Green Eagle, a slender but tall Caucasian sporting one of those long, scraggly red beards that grows unchecked to just below the eyes. Reportedly, he had been adopted and trained in this practice by the Cheyenne Nation, one of the more severe custodians of such traditions it turns out. Under the stars and his solemn, purposeful direction, we collected many large pre-cut chunks of wood, carefully piling them around and over a stack of thirty or so football-sized rocks piled about ten feet in front of the sweat lodge. Kindling was then placed in four spots, corresponding to the four compass points, and ignited. Three hours later, just as the sun was rising, the rocks had acquired the necessary orange glow from absorbing the bonfire's heat, which prompted Green Eagle to action. With a polished pitchfork-shaped ceremonial staff, he carefully placed ten of these rocks in the pit through the one small doorway in the lodge, which was exposed by pulling back a loose flap of tarp. We filed in, one at a time, in a clock-wise direction. Clothing was optional, and most people, including myself, wore at least shorts of some kind, not so much for the sake of modesty, but because the ground cover around the pit inside the lodge was straw. Green Eagle was the first to enter so he ended up by the right side of the opening where he could control the flap. Once we were squeezed in, side by sweaty side, he pulled the flap shut, sealing off all air and light.

I knew roughly what was going to happen, having person-ally talked to at least two known survivors. There were to be four "rounds," as they are called, of twenty to thirty minutes each. In between rounds the flap would be opened for about five minutes to let in fresh air and to put more hot rocks in the pit. Each round signified a specific aspect of the ritual. The first round was for getting in touch with any troubling emo-tions. The second was to let go of anything getting in our way of clarity. The third was for "visioning," accomplished by surrendering to the Great Spirit. The fourth was to give thanks and to mentally bring anyone we wanted into the lodge to receive a blessing. It sounded easy enough; and I really wasn't too worried, having often frequented the saunas in local health spas.

I was immediately struck by how dark it became as Green Eagle pulled the flap shut with the coarse scraping sound of sliding canvas, which caused me some momentary disappointment because the woman to my left was rather nice looking and, even though completely dedicated to this quest, I had figured if I got bored I could pass the time by watching perspiration glide down the more interesting parts of her body. Recovering from that loss, I shut my eyes and began to meditate while Green Eagle dipped an ornate, gourd ladle into the water bucket at his side and flung its contents onto the shimmering rocks, which immediately hissed and sizzled loudly to mark the official beginning of the sweat. Like everyone else, I was touching shoulders with two other people in the cramped quarters, which, after letting go of my initial worry about underarm deodorant protection, felt reassuring. To this point, it felt pretty much like a typical sauna; however, as a succession of five or six more ladlefuls of water dowsed the hot rocks, a cloud of hissing steam rose quickly to the top of the lodge and then rolled down in all directions along the inside of the heavy canvas.

As the boiling mist enveloped my face, the heat was more intense than anything I had ever experienced. The air coming into my nostrils felt like fire and completely prevented any further breathing. Beginning to gasp, I immediately realized that someone had obviously made a dreadful mistake. Green Eagle couldn't have meant for it to be this hot. I bent completely over so that my head was close to the ground where, theoretically, the air was cooler. After several painful attempts, I was able to take a few breaths in somewhat of a normal rhythm. Modesty prevailing, I didn't want to be the first to address Green Eagle about the inferno he had created; but I was sure someone would at any second, so I prepared myself to firmly support the slightest voiced concern. After about five minutes, just as the muffled gasps and pants from around the circle began to subside and the opportunity for an objective discussion appeared imminent, Green Eagle began throwing more water on the pulsating rocks, initiating another shower of searing steam. At this point I had a choice of either taking a deep breath of relatively cool air and holding it until the on-coming wave of angry vapor passed or using that breath to ask the question if anyone else was concerned about being further scalded. As much for vanity's sake as for survival, I choose the former, retaining my breath and my protests.

With my head now pressed solidly against the ground-straw in a rather awkward but necessary position to eventually again breathe, I suddenly realized the logic for the most important rule of the sweat, which had been emphasized by Green Eagle several times prior to our entering the lodge—"No pissing once inside." I could just picture what would happen if someone did and it seeped down onto the hot rocks to become "yellow steam" in these cramped quarters. Obviously, this was a cardinal law, not just because such a foul odor would disrupt the ceremony, but because it would provide the tormented group with an irresistible excuse to mutiny.

Green Eagle then reminded us that the purpose of this ritual was purification. Supposedly, only those aspects that need purification would react to the heat. Whenever pain was experienced, the thoughts and feelings at those moments were the "toxins" of the Spirit. As they were released, the body would also release its discomfort, merely allowing the searing heat to pass right through. This process could help one identify and then let go of any unwanted emotions.

By the end of the first round I had a headache, not to mention blistered lips and irritated, tearing eyes. Much to my annoyance, the heat was obviously not passing through me without effect. However, it was now a matter of pride for me to endure. Even though I had thoughts of unceremoniously darting out whenever the flap was periodically opened, I persevered and even participated in the chanting and sharing throughout the entire sweat, which seemed to last a lot longer than the stated two hours. (Sweats done in accordance with tribal customs other than Cheyenne allow for the "sweatees" to cool off outside the lodge in between rounds. It was fortunate for Green Eagle that most of us only found out about this acceptable variation a day or two after this sweat was concluded, when he was safely beyond our reach.)

Upon leaving the lodge, most of us staggered to a nearby stream and plopped our proud but exhausted bodies into the cool water. Then we regathered as a group, shared some impressions, and went our separate ways. I did feel exceptionally clean from this purifying ordeal, but it was hard to say exactly what had been purged other than all my energy. Having anticipated an immediate and unmistakable soul-cleansing result, I was probably feeling a little let down. This disappointment, plus my weakened physical condition, are the only excuses I have for what transpired next.

•   •   •

Harbon Hot Springs sported a bulletin board gazebo in the middle of their grounds to which announcements of various bizarre events were posted. As I trudged passed it with the intention of disappearing into a comfortable sleeping bag in the back of my truck, one colorful flier in particular caught my attention. It was another one of those seminars that, when reading the title, made my body become rigid—"Fire Dancing."

Now, I had heard of fire-walking seminars like the one put on by the infamous Tony Robbins, but fire dancing? Just the thought of doing it scared me silly, not just of being burned, but also possibly of "chickening out" at the moment of truth in front of everyone. There was nothing logical about putting myself in such an apparent no-win position; yet there I was again, wondering if I should. Here was yet another process of purification presenting itself. If I ignored it, I might miss out on learning the very thing that would enable me to forgive Dawyn. . . . Since the seminar was scheduled to start in a couple hours, and it was probably too late to attend, I decided to leave the decision to providence. I simply didn't count on the sponsoring organization to be so unprofessional as to allow participants to actually sign up at the very start of the event.

In agreeing to attend this seminar where I would be walking, or dancing, on burning coals that reach the temperature of 1500 degrees, I didn't think it unreasonable to expect the seminar leader to be one who instilled confidence. This need was all the more evident when I met the other eleven fidgety people who had converged with as much apprehension as myself, also masked by a similar nervous alacrity. Imagine my surprise when one of these very anxious people stood up and introduced herself as Charity, our leader. Unfortunately, at this point I had already paid my money.

We spent an hour or so in a circle talking about why each of us had come and our fears about doing such a crazy thing. Then we walked about a half mile to a meadow where a large circular area had been outlined in stones to designate it as a ritual site. All of us participated in building a huge pyre-like mound of wood from the several stacked cords of oak and bay. The plan was to light the pile of wood, which we did, and all go back to the lodge to do some mental processes designed to create the frame of mind needed for this feat to be successful and then eat dinner. The fire would take about three or four hours to create the required glowing embers. For no apparent reason, I volunteered to stay with the fire tender, a pixie-type fellow from Guatemala who spoke little English.

About three hours later the group returned along with some people from a nearby seminar who had heard of this folly and were intrigued to watch. The coals were spread in roughly a rectangular design about ten feet wide and twenty feet long. Taking off our shoes and socks, about twenty-five of us stood in a circle, surrounding this pulsating orange carpet with numerous flashes of little yellowish flames poking up from between the darker spots to wave. The ground was damp and, with the sun gone, was also very cold. This was at first an annoying distraction to me, but I soon learned that the near-frozen mud gave an added incentive to take that crucial first step onto the coals. Everyone was watching Charity, who appeared to be just about ready to initiate the proceedings when she abruptly turned away from the fire, picked up her clip board, and hurried over to me. Ever alert, I quickly braced myself thinking for an instant that possibly she had decided to enter the fire from my particular position and might, in her haste, inadvertently take me with her. Instead she had suddenly remembered that I had not signed a liability release form. Having dispatched of that chore, she returned to her designed point of entry to give final instructions.

"The first time we go through the fire. . . ."

"The first time?" I almost said out loud in a surprised, puzzled voice. "There is a very large presumption here," I thought to myself.

". . . . should be done in silence. After everyone's had an opportunity to go through once, then the musicians will start playing. . . ."

I had wondered where those three guys with conga drums had come from. Since they hadn't taken off their shoes like the rest of us, I thought they were just odd-looking locals from the nearby campground, curious about this strange barbecue.

". . . . Remember, just say to yourself that your body will do whatever it needs to protect itself, and then walk at your normal pace across the fire. . . ."

"Not 'cool moss?'" I asked myself. I knew Tony Robbins used the term "cool moss." Evidently, saying this phrase over and over again when walking across the coals could change the brain's interpretation of the sensations being sent by the feet, no matter how unpleasant they might be.

". . . . I don't want anyone to be into denial. Do not deny that you are walking on fire. You **are** walking on fire. Your body can and will protect itself even when walking or dancing on fire. Acknowledge it, and it will purify you. . . ."

I got it—just affirm that it's real fire and that my body will protect itself. Okay, I could do that. So, to myself and with my eyes closed I followed her instructions. Unfortunately, when I opened my eyes and again saw the forbidding glow of the coals and felt their bellowing heat, my stomach returned to its natural state of nauseous knots. In a panicky attempt at self-hypnosis, I began repeating to myself, "I will protect myself; walk naturally." Unfortunately, long before I could effectively go unconscious, the ceremony began.

Charity stepped to the very edge of the fire and hesitated with her eyes closed, as if saying a prayer just to be on the safe side. Then, without further ceremony she bolted onto the coals. Granted, I had only known her for a few hours, but I suddenly saw her rather robust frame moving faster than at any previous time. In five steps she was over the twenty foot bed of coals and standing with both feet in a bucket of water. (Having a bucket of water nearby is evidently standard procedure to put out any embers that might get embedded between the toes or to dowse any clothes that might catch on fire.)

The group began rotating around the coals counterclockwise as, one at a time, each person took a deep breath and grimly followed the path our leader had blazed, most approximating her so-called normal lope and some moving even faster. I graciously let a few people pass me by as I approached the actual point of embarkation. Watching the others go across the burning coals, I rationalized that, reflexes being what they are, no one probably felt anything until they were all the way through, at which time any painful sensations that just happened to get through the body's protection would catch up to them. So, any grimaces I might make as my feet were being grilled would occur once I was at the bucket and away from group scrutiny, but even that thought was of dubious value as I tried to corral my courage.

Finally, I was there. I stepped to the edge and my gaze fell to the center of the fire. I could sense everyone looking at me. One or two others had already declined to go, stepping to one side and opting to think about it a little longer. I knew it wouldn't be the end of the world if I followed that course. As I concentrated once more on the programmed litany about self-protection, fear flooded through me, short-circuiting any meaningful mental activity. It seemed like I was still debating my options when I suddenly realized, in terror, that my right foot had lifted into the air and was heading forward. Momentum was now in charge; I was committed.

That first step onto the coals brought with it an instant realization—I probably should have gone to the "cool moss" seminar where I could have remained in conditioned denial. And, had Wide World of Sports been timing everyone in this event, undoubtedly I would have finished in the top three; but I somehow didn't feel badly about that. In fact, as I scooted over the embers and hurriedly thrust my feet into the bucket of cold water, I felt elated. All the fear and uncertainty was now gone. I honestly felt like dancing, and I was obviously not alone in my reaction. As the primal sounds of drumming started, people began walking across the coals again and again, letting the primitive rhythm control their movements. The pace slowed and some even did twirls and figure eights on their journey from one side to the other. I managed to samba with this Fire God three times and thoroughly enjoyed watching a few others chalk up a dozen or so crossings. Surprisingly, in addition to their incredible heat, the coals had a texture, something like popcorn, and emitted a little crunch with each step. I kept wondering if my feet were being burned. They were aching, but I couldn't tell if that was because of the extremely cold water and the near frozen ground, or because they were approaching medium rare.

Back in our dormitory-style room, the entire group stayed up talking for quite a while using up our excess adrenaline. The theory holds that if the feet get burned it is a sign that there is an emotional block relating to something else going on in life. It was an interesting sight, all of us sitting around talking about how great it felt to go through our fears and at the same time trying to inconspicuously examine the soles of our feet to check for emerging blisters. None of us wanted to admit the possibility that we couldn't protect ourselves, even though blisters are apparently quite common in these seminars. As I began to warm up and the pain did not go away in my feet, I became convinced I had indeed burned them. I was very surprised and happy with myself to awaken in the morning not having any blisters.

After a well-deserved hearty breakfast, I quickly packed my stuff in the truck. I did somehow feel purified and lighter in spirit from the events of the previous day. "Now I can forgive Dawyn," I said to myself with some degree of pride as I start driving down the long, windy gravel road to the highway fork.

"Who are you to forgive Dawyn?"

If anything I expected some acknowledgment, hopefully praise, but certainly not recrimination from my inner "friend;" so I naturally reacted accordingly. "I'm the guy that's just gone through a whole day of fire torture to get to this point of contrition, that's who."

"So, now you can forgive Dawyn for betraying you?"

"I think maybe I can now, yeah."

"Did you ever consider that the act of forgiveness is really just another way to justify your original condemnation?"

"What? No, I've never considered that, and I'm not sure I want to."

"Let's take this by the numbers. First, Dawyn does something that, in your eyes, is wrong, so you get angry with her, right?"

"She did do something wrong."

"Second, you feel justified wallowing in your anger for a while because of what she did."

"Well, I wouldn't say I wallowed."

"Third, you see that your anger really isn't doing anything except creating problems in your own life, so you decide that maybe it's time to rise above this betrayal and forgive her."

"Well, I can see how one might possibly look at it that way but. . . ."

"Fourth, you undertake some arduous process to underscore how powerful your anger is and how much effort it's taking on your part to overcome it."

"I don't think I like where this is headed."

"Fifth, in a final magnanimous gesture, you declare yourself free from that justified burden of anger and grant Dawyn forgiveness for her terrible sins."

"Well, I really wasn't going to make too big a deal out of it. Probably ask her to lunch and. . . ."

"Every step of this process, including the act of forgiveness, declares that Dawyn was wrong, that she deserved your condemnation in the first place. If she didn't, why would you need to forgive her?"

"Why didn't we have this conversation yesterday morning before my apparently unnecessary excursions into the upper ranges of the Fahrenheit scale?"

"Because it was important for you to get to this point in order to see the fallacy of forgiveness. Forgiving Dawyn feels right to you now, just as condemning her felt right before. But, don't let it blind you to the fact that your judging Dawyn was the sole cause of this entire emotional cycle."

"My judging her? I was just observing and reacting. She lied, and I certainly have a right to establish standards for my relationships; and not being lied to is one of those standards."

"Why did she lie?"

"Because she's. . . selfish. . . and. . . ." At this point I realized that some ways back I had turned East on Highway 112 when I meant to turn West, but I decided to keep going until I could casually make a U-turn without it becoming an unwanted topic of this dialogue.

"You don't really understand why she did what she did, do you?"

"I can guess."

"And your guesses turned into judgments, and these judgments prevented your from truly understanding her."

"I knew I wasn't going to like this conversation."

"Do you want to understand or do you want to feel righteous? . . . Do you want to keep going in the wrong direction, or can you let go of your pride?"

As soon as I heard it, I knew that was the million dollar question, and I also realized there was no point in waiting to turn the truck around. I pulled onto the shoulder of the road, let the car behind me go by, and then swung an abrupt U-turn. My greatest satisfaction over the past months of depression had been knowing I was right and she was wrong. Several miles of familiar scenery went by before I answered. "Yeah, I do want to understand."

"Okay, let's look at exactly what she did to upset you."

"All right, if we're going to start there, I've got a chance to win this argument," I thought to myself for encouragement. "I heard her commit to loving me unconditionally and creating a life together, and then she withdrew from the relationship. . . and didn't even tell me why," I declared with authority.

"And this is what you don't understand."

"Yeah, I don't understand why she did it, and why it's not important enough for her to even look at."

"Prior to Dawyn, had you ever told anyone you loved them?"

I began to get that sinking feeling, again. "Well. . . ."

"That you loved them totally and would love them forever?"

". . . . eh. . . yeah. . . ."

"And did you happen to withdraw from any of these relationships?"

I began seeing a succession of questioning faces belonging to the women who had heard those words from me, and believed them, and trusted them, and eventually felt betrayed. I was silent, as resistive tears began to well in my eyes. I had never deliberately lied to any of them; I truly did love them when I told them so, but somehow it never worked out the way I pictured it should. I was always hoping the "I love you" would last forever. I guess I thought that if I could just say it often enough it would come true. . . but always it would fade and again be time to search for my soulmate. . . .

"And, did you ever tell them why your love died?"

I don't think I knew why exactly, or if I did I didn't want to look at it. They stopped fitting the ideal of that special person I wanted, and I needed to get on to finding the one that would. How do you tell someone you don't love her anymore simply because she's not Laura Petrie? . . . Quite a while went by as I drove in that heavy silence. I felt a thick cloud of guilt forming, for there seemed to be so many people with whom I had travelled this relationship road.

"Were you wrong for doing what you did?"

"I guess we're getting to the easy questions, now. Of course I was."

"Just like Dawyn was wrong."

"Guess we both were," I concluded, finally seeing the point.

"The only problem is you weren't wrong; you were just being yourself. Everything you did you thought was the right thing to do at the time, and each of your choices has helped guide you in some way to your present level of understanding. And the same is true for Dawyn."

"So, I don't need to forgive her?"

"If you judge Dawyn as not being lovable, thereby blocking your love from flowing to her, it is not Dawyn that needs forgiving. She has no control over your judgements. . . ."

Painfully, the logic to what I was hearing began to sink in. "Well, somebody should be forgiven! I mean look at all the pain that resulted."

"Without judgement, there is no such concept as forgiveness. . . . You both were simply making the best choices you could on your respective journeys."

I started to ask why I had gone through this whole forgiveness struggle, but the answer was obvious—it was the only way I could release it. In a strange, benign way I felt close to Dawyn once more and let myself recall her distinct laugh, which always warmed my heart.

By the time I got home I was actually glad I had gone through these tests by fire. They had brought up things that were hard for me to look at, but I felt as if my typical convoluted thinking was really starting to unravel and beginning to free me from past patterns. It was obvious that taking advantage of these strange situations presenting themselves, although they physically pushed me and challenged my beliefs, not to mention my emotional limits, was beneficial in my quest for hidden truths. They would also make great literary copy if I could ultimately make sense of it all. Insights of various shapes and sizes seemed to be ever-present of late. It was the process of integrating them into my life to experience their truth that was proving to be difficult. Mistakenly thinking I could now use the next few months to digest these most recent experiences, I casually punched the button on the answering machine to be greeted by an unusual, but enthusiastic, message from a buddy.

"Do you know anything about Shamanism?"

Consuming most of the thirty minute cassette, the communication contained an elaborate description of a fourteen-day trek through the Grand Canyon on rafts hosted by a mysterious Native American Shaman Priestess from Montana. I listened patiently, noticing a variety of feelings arising within me throughout the narration: I liked river rafting and had always been intrigued by this natural geographic wonder of the Southwest; but at the same time I was somewhat fearful of what I had heard about the rapids on the Colorado River; and I was more than a little cautious of Shamanism, no doubt a result of traditional religious inculcations while growing up. Even though I had just reconfirmed my intention to take advantage of any learning opportunities that crossed my path, I saw no compelling reason to rush into this particular one—until I heard the last few words of the message:

". . . . fifteen people max on the trip and there's only one slot left. By the way, thirteen of those signed up are women."

•   •   •

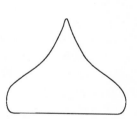

Gems of wisdom, like the fruits that grow,
Are offered by peddlers, right and left,
But a harvested truth from what others sow,
Is as foolish as the blind reading to the deaf.

Chapter Ten

The Course of the Explorer

Two weeks later, I was standing excitedly in the dry desert air of the upper Grand Canyon in Northern Arizona. I must admit that I relished a certain amount of anticipation as the group gathered at Harper's Ferry, a relatively level pile of rocks and sand so named for an ingenious nineteenth century entrepreneur who stretched a cable across this shallow spot of the Colorado River and charged people to pull themselves across. Shamanism, the general term given to the practice of using "magic" to connect with the unseen forces and realms of nature, held a wonderful mystique for me. I suppose my quickened pulse was also somewhat a result of the generous feminine ratio and the seemingly ever present premonition that I was going to meet that special someone where the choice for a soulmate relationship would be mutual. Besides, four-to-one odds had to be the Universe finally smiling on this humble and deserving student.

The women were members of a Montana organization that sponsored self-awareness-type events, especially in the sacred American Indian tradition. Knowing I was from California, they were naturally a little wary of me as our four-raft flotilla began; however, after a few days of listening to my harrowing sagas of the sweat lodge and fire dancing rituals, they readily welcomed me into their daily ceremony, simply referred to as "the Circle."

These evening rituals were presided over by a petite group leader, the Shaman Priestess, who was physically very strong and often made good use of a rather penetrating, dark-eyed stare. Following her lead, we would beat make-shift drums and sporadically chant until someone in the circle would suddenly became emotional, usually to the point of appearing possessed and actually needing to be sat upon by several others until exorcised, which was accomplished by the priestess encouraging the possessee to writhe vigorously and emit loud guttural screams. This seemed to be of some benefit to the one afflicted but did little to endear our expedition to the benevolent wildlife living along the acoustically sensitive canyon, not to mention other groups of voyagers camped nearby who always seemed to give us a wide berth when passing on the river.

In general, I had considered Shamanism to be a rather shadowy, secretive practice, conducted by shady characters who didn't talk too much, sported enigmatic smiles, and cast spells the way most folks send greeting cards. Although, having read all about Don Juan and Don Genero, the avuncular Shaman in the Castaneda books, I knew such encounters were not always fatal. But, even with all of my premonitions, I quickly found myself going out of my way to look for more intrigue. This Shaman Priestess, aside from the official ceremonies, remained aloof the entire trip. She explained at one point that she was preoccupied, and I assumed from her expression and posture at the time that she was locked in mortal combat with another dark force somewhere in another realm. So other things began to occupy my attention.

All the rapids fluctuated in difficulty depending on which dam operator upstream happened to be manning the flow valve several hours earlier. Our usual course of action was to pull ashore just ahead of a major rapids and have everyone "scout it" while the guides pointed out the "line" through the churning roar that appeared safest. We would also quickly go over the plan of action in case one of the four rubber boats flipped; but, since that hadn't happened so far, we quickly finished the regular routine at Hanns Rapids and shoved off. About half way through this one particular stretch of angry agitation, the raft I happened to be on was casually tossed atop one of the many menacing bus-sized boulders randomly positioned throughout the long, sloping tumult—this occurring in spite of a carefully planned route by our guide and a most extraordinary exhibition of frenzied but chaotic paddling from the rest of us on board. Evidently not content with just isolating us in this completely unreachable spot from either shore, the river suddenly produced a gushing torrent of icy water over the raft's now submerged stern, abruptly insisting that our guide, the only one among us capable of steering, continue downstream by herself.

The other rafts, having already made it safely through, quickly pulled over and, after taking a few minutes to help our embarrassed and shivering guide to safety, raced up river on foot and began trying to yell instructions through the deafening din of rushing water to the six of us still marooned. At least that's what we assumed was the object of our animated comrades ashore because we could see their lips moving while we watched with some degree of concern their many valiant but unsuccessful attempts to throw us a line. Just about the time our nervous laughter was fading into panic, the river capriciously lifted the raft off the rock and spun us through the rest of the rapids in a fashion not unlike the Mad Hatter Teacup ride. One of our would-be rescuers had the presence of mind (and malicious nature) to record the entire event on film through a telescopic lens; and, although the pictures weren't seen until a month later, the wonderful expressions on our faces during the ordeal portrayed a much different experience than the "all in a day's work" confidence we conveyed later that night around the campfire.

It is possible that such harrowing experiences stimulate amorous inclinations because, right after that, I actually found myself with a slight attraction toward the Shaman Priestess herself. However she was fairly oblivious to anyone not in need of demonic abatement. To snare her attention, I thought briefly about faking a few contortions and tremors during one of our nightly Circles, but quickly discarded that errant idea when counting at least three full-figured women in the group whom I would not want sitting on me for any reason—not even an exorcism.

Another promising though fleeting romantic possibility arose when I noticed the engaging smile and loving nature of the expedition's beautiful, dark-haired cook. For a couple of days she and I spent some lazy hours talking and joking, heading for what I thought was that special moment of understanding, and I guess it was a special cognition of sorts. Her affinity and trust for me developed to the point where she shared her fears of men. However, in the course of this soul-searching dialogue, she discovered she was more attracted to feminine than male characteristics and, delighted with the clarity of that insight, developed an immediate attraction for another woman in the group, with whom she then spent the remainder of the trip. I quickly rationalized that it was certainly better for me to find this out now rather than after I had said or done something that revealed my vulnerability.

On the next to last day of the trip, I walked up a side wash that led to the west end of Havesu Canyon, still sacred land of the Hopi Indians and easily one of the most beautiful places on Earth. Here at Moon Falls, a year-round waterfall drops two-hundred feet over a white limestone cliff into a brilliant turquoise pool. Then the warm stream meanders through a series of countless smaller falls over the next five miles until it surrenders to the rush of the Colorado River, which seems to collect it without notice. Sitting alone on the sun-bleached rocks I felt myself, as the Warrior, anxious to discover the next step, whatever that might be.

•   •   •

In addition to being expensive both in terms of money and time, this limited encounter with Shamanism had not proved to be terribly enlightening. Although I remained convinced that continuing to explore the many converging though unusual teachings appearing along my current path was the right direction for my Spirit's Journey, it was obvious I needed to be more discriminating in what I chose. By the time I arrived home from Arizona, I had compiled a tentative list of about thirty various and diverse disciplines to possibly pursue as part of this exploration.

Over the next few months I delved into a half dozen or so, and all in their own way proved to be interesting and informative though quite insistent of my time. I began to get the discouraging feeling that I would find an inordinate consumption of that commodity was required by all these teachings. Calculating the approximate days needed to acquire an expertise in just a few of these areas took me well past the year 2050, at which point the information would probably be of dubious use to me anyway. Before I went any further it was time to find out which of these would really be of help. Waking up early one day, I postponed my usual writing schedule to see what my "friend" had to offer.

"Nice to hear from you again." Its tone was loving; and if there was a hidden hint of sarcasm in reference to my not communicating of late, I missed it.

"Can you help me out here?" I began while picking up my list in anticipation of having to read it.

"Well, looks like you're entering the phase of the Explorer."

Hearing that got me initially excited. "That's welcome news. . . I think. What does the Explorer do?"

"As the Warrior, you release fears and begin to experience aspects of your life beyond what your identity-based reality can account for. Relying mainly on your emerging intuition, you develop an insatiable appetite to explore and discover all paths to truth, to who you really are. You tend to see things with your heart rather than your logic, and your primary emotional states are excitement and exhilaration."

I smiled with some justifiable pride. "So, which one of these disciplines will be of greatest help to me in discovering more of the truth?

"All of them. . . and none of them. . . ."

"I should have known. Ask a simple question, get back two simple answers."

"Virtually every discipline on your list could provide the valuable experiences and insights you seek."

"That's what I figured, but certainly one or two of them would take less time to. . . ."

"However, just as each can facilitate your development, each has the ample ability to prevent your growth."

"What?" I figured a couple might turn out to be red herrings, but all of them able to screw me up?

"The real danger is the temptation to rely on these outside interpretations rather than developing and trusting your own intuitive ability to know the truths of the Universe, which by the way present themselves to you every moment."

"So, I shouldn't bother studying any of 'em?"

"You're hoping to find the answers to your own confusion by exposing yourself to what others believe."

"Well, yeah. No sense reinventing the wheel. And, there may be one discipline or teacher that has just the piece of the puzzle I need."

"Everyone is born with the same inherent ability to some-how make their own way up the mountain. This means that an Aborigine tribesman, a Rhodes' scholar, and you all have the same chance to attain enlightenment. Now, do you think there's an Aborigine tribesman out there in the bush right now pondering whether to spend the next year of his life studying Zen or Numerology?"

Although its logic was admirable, because of its tone I did not feel the question warranted an answer. Instead, I quickly scratched those two disciplines off my list while casually looking away to think.

"The value of pursuing another's truth is not the knowledge it may contain, but rather the knowledge already within you that it may trigger and reveal. The discipline to follow is the one that will assist you in removing the internal blocks to your own natural power—your own natural state of intuitive knowledge."

"But, don't some of them, like say Astrology or Tantra Yoga, contain valuable information that can help me on this journey?"

"Tantra, huh? Sounds like those testosterone levels are getting high again?"

I felt a slight blush at being so obvious. "Okay, so I tried to slip one past you. Just Astrology, then. Doesn't it explain the forces that control my life?"

"Unless you will it, either consciously or unconsciously, there is no force in the Universe that can control you. Did you not experience this truth when fire dancing?"

I reflexively looked at my feet and curled my toes. "Okay, let's say for the sake of argument that I don't need any of these teachings, but that some could help me more than others?"

"Alright."

"So, which one would be the right choice to assist me at this point in my life?"

"When you put it that way, then there is one that would be the right choice."

"Okay. Now we're getting somewhere. Which one?" I prepared to do some underlining on my list.

"Whichever one you choose, of course."

I unconsciously began tapping my fingers on the computer mouse pad. "Of course! But, what if I choose the wrong one and. . . ."

"You can't make the wrong choice. You never have."

That caught me off guard. Of course I'd made wrong choices, all the ones that ended in pain for me and others.

"Every decision, every action, every thought and emotion in your life has been exactly what it had to be to get you to this moment. In fact, being who you are, you couldn't have made any other choices. . . ."

I stopped fidgeting. "But, what about when it turned out to be a disaster?"

"Let's say you make a choice and end up running into a brick wall, at which point you could say you took the wrong path. However, taking this so-called disastrous path has given you the opportunity to learn two important things. The first is that the direction you took is not the right one for you. Secondly, it provides the opportunity to look back at yourself standing at that decision point in the road and understand why you weren't tuned in to your intuitive voice that was telling you to take the other path. Learning these two things was obviously what you needed to do; therefore you made the right choice after all."

This idea conveyed an unexpected but temporary sense of comfort amid my frustration. "Okay, I get that. But aren't there some objective ways to evaluate these forks in the road rather than relying on trial and error?" My tone was one notch short of pleading, as I had visions of spending the next several years learning the many valuable lessons of all the paths that don't work for me."

"Sure."

"You mean I'm going to get a direct answer!" I sighed to myself.

"If the teaching holds that you absolutely need what it offers to discover yourself, than it is not honoring your inherent ability to know the truth on your own. Teachings that foster your own intuitive abilities are likely to provide more opportunities for you to discover yourself."

"Okay, let me get this down." I started scribbling some notes.

"Any teaching that asks you to focus on what your life should be is just encouraging the development of more pictures in your mind. Having such pictures keeps your attention focussed on what isn't there, rather than on what is, taking your attention out of the moment. All power for self-discovery lies only in the moment."

My fingers were hurting. This was like spending hours trying to get the cork out and then having the champagne foam out faster than I could drink it.

"Also, any teaching that purports to be a truth will allow for all other truths, and it will never discount what you experience as the truth."

I stopped trying to take notes. As was customary in these conversations, what I was hearing surprised me and at the same time seemed like very familiar common-sense.

"Those who just seek to inspire are often those who have hidden doubts, and their need is for you to believe in them so that they don't have to face these doubts. Do they seek to empower you, or do they desire for you to empower them? Are they content with the natural harmony and joy that connects all people, or do they request the use of your resources to achieve their own destiny? Teachers who truly embrace the Spirit's Journey and from whom others learn the most are those who let their daily actions speak their loudest truths. . . . Is this the information you wanted?"

Recognizing the unmistakable chide, I laughed and shook my head while returning to some final quick notes.

"Maybe the next teaching to pursue would be easier to select if you decided what area of yourself you'd like to explore?"

I didn't answer, and I don't think it expected one. I had been using the tried and true "shotgun approach" to self-discovery without much thought as to any target within me. But there was one area of greatest interest. If my Magician had established an identity that concealed me, and my Wanderer had sensed there was more to me than that identity, and my Warrior had pushed through the fears of that identity, and now my Explorer was beginning to discover things beyond that identity, who was this "me" behind them all? Which teaching could help me truly discover this? Little did I realize that the direction for that answer was not even on my extensive list.

•   •   •

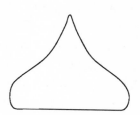

Beneath the dreams, and all the desire,
Behind the thoughts, and all the emotion,
Shining through the layers like eternal fire,
Burns a singular flame in quiet devotion.

Chapter Eleven

The Pearl of Essence

"Extraterrestrials! As in 'E.T.'?" I responded incredulously.

I really didn't know Sabina well enough to distinguish if she was putting me on or really was genuinely excited to the point of what looked like the beginning stages of an orgasm. Being trained in physical therapy as well as operatic singing, she occasionally attempted to rejuvenate my body and also construct some discipline around my willing but aberrant voice, courageous endeavors that had begun to mold a strong friendship between us over the last few months. I had dropped by her house on a whim, using some pretext of copying a music tape, I think, only to discover that she had recently spent a week with some people in Arizona who claimed to be extraterrestrials. It evidently had been the pivotal experience of her life, enough so that she was off the next day to attend another of their gatherings. Recognizing Sabina to be dedicated to her own spiritual path and a thoroughly honest person, I listened politely but didn't take her rosy impressions too seriously, having encountered many opportunists on this journey who specialize in acquiring such enthusiastic accolades. It was mostly out of curiosity that I agreed to watch the E.T.'s promotional video she just happened to have, which I found boring.

Aside from the bright glow in Sabina's eyes as she anticipated seeing them again, nothing about this "alien" situation even seemed remotely applicable to my current quest. So I was left with no explanation for my undeniable impulse to accompany her—except for the fact that Sabina was extremely sensual and, being in the natural romance of the high desert country, there was the increased possibility of giving our mutual but unspoken attraction to each other the opportunity to blossom. I wasn't especially proud of again giving in to this prurient instinct; however, I had been assured that I would find true love on my journey and who's to say that couldn't happen sooner than later? Besides, maybe I was closer to the end than I thought.

As for the literary portion of my life, the timing couldn't have been better seeing that I had completed a typed draft of my latest manuscript, cleverly titled *The Game of Mystery,* and delivered it two weeks earlier into the hands of several "readers" who were to give me valuable feedback for any minor changes that possibly might be needed, while at the same time enriching their own lives immeasurably. The book's premise was simple, yet intriguing—life is both a mystery and a game. The mystery is, "Who am I?" When we think we have solved that mystery, we begin playing the game, "This is who I am." When we begin to lose at playing this game, we immediately go back to solving more of the mystery. This was obviously a great work, begging to be published; and I had anticipated receiving the copies back from these lucky readers within a few days, along with some small notes of appreciation and appropriate praise, of course. Unfortunately, when the manuscripts did arrive, all but one of the people who had agreed to expose themselves to my cogent observations were unable to make it past the first chapter without taking more than the manufacturer's recommended dosage of aspirin. And evidently none of the readers got far enough into the treatise to benefit from any of my truly sage commentary, cleverly hidden in the middle chapters. (This last assumption may be premature in that two of the readers have yet to return my phone calls with their progress.) Although I took some solace from their exulting testimonials, which ranged from "nice" to "very convoluted," it was disheartening to see this country's neglect of quality literature coming so close to my doorstep.

After further reflection on their critiques, I realized I obviously had given steak to those used to hamburger; but, even with all my training in human nature, I was still taken back by the insidious and pervasive effect envy can have on otherwise decent people. Seeing that it would serve no useful purpose to confront them about this character flaw, I simply identified a few other truly objective people I knew who had matured emotionally enough to review this literary milestone without succumbing to base jealousy. Distributing this second batch just that very day before chancing upon Sabina, I was free for another adventure, confident that upon my return I would have a valid set of opinions on my book. So I agreed to meet her there.

The drive from San Francisco to Sedona, Arizona took about sixteen hours. Eight hours into the trip, around midnight, I turned off busy Highway 5 onto the deserted Interstate 51 toward Barstow. As I started to pick up speed after obliging the off-ramp stop sign, a large, white owl flew through my headlights, dangerously close to the right fender and glided to a majestic moon-lit pose on a grey, weathered fence post about thirty feet off the road, letting its head swivel to watch me go by. I admired its grace and merely accepted the close encounter as a good omen before returning my attention to the radio in a vain attempt to locate a non-country/western station.

Because I arrived at the split-level house overlooking downtown Sedona before Sabina, none of the seven curious faces were familiar to me as I entered, sleeping bag and suitcase in tow. These people seemed normal, though, so I went about my business of staking out a corner in one of the downstairs bedrooms. All told, there were eighteen of us who planned to share this three bedroom, two bath dwelling for the next four days. The first "session" of the seminar wasn't scheduled to start for another half hour, so I began to mingle.

In the large living room scattered with sofas and pillows, I sat down next to an intense looking guy in his twenties. I had briefly noticed him earlier engaged in animated conversation, so I figured he'd be easy to talk to.

"I'm Kosh-Kar," was his deliberate but friendly response as I introduced myself.

I wasn't too surprised that people were using their nick names. It had appeared to me when I entered that most everyone knew each other, somewhat like a reunion of sorts. I thought he said "crash car," but since he did not impress me as being the race car type, I asked for clarification.

"No, Kosh-Kar, K-O-S-H-K-A-R. Actually it's Kosh-Kar Malovia. You haven't got your name yet, I guess."

Ah ha! It was some sort of game to come up with a different name. All I had to do was discover the rules for devising this alias and I'd be set. I liked games with a clever challenge. "No, just the one I came with."

He nodded with a patient smile.

"What do you do?" I was going to stay fairly traditional until I could decipher the process.

"I put on seminars with Altrinia." He quickly glanced away, pointing with his eyes toward a lady, probably in her late thirties, with a very kind and distant countenance.

"Oh, what kind of seminars?" I let a little excitement spill out anticipating we had something in common.

"Mostly the programs of Vector Three, accessing the Akashic Records, time travel in our Light Bodies, stuff like that. . . ."

It was right about here that I began regretting my not having asked Sabina a few more specifics about this event. "How long have you been teaching these seminars?"

"Altrinia and I are really just putting this particular one together; but heck, I've been doin' them for. . . ten thousand years now. . . but not always on this planet, though."

I nodded and quickly looked around in hopes of finding some munchies. "Hey, that's sounds great. Do you have a brochure or flier?"

"Altrinia has them.""Be sure to give me one before this is over, okay? I'm going to get one of those mineral waters I see everyone drinking." My apprehensive exit to the kitchen was pretty smooth I thought, at least for someone who suddenly felt it would be extremely unwise to expose his back to anyone in this group. Retrieving a full bottle of Evian water from the kitchen, I headed for an empty chair at the dining room table where a group of four women and one man were conversing. This was much better. I could just casually observe and listen for awhile, maybe pick up some clues to the game that would help me come up with a suitable nickname. Sitting down unobserved, I guessed that the man must be sporting an earring, as everyone had paused to examine that part of his anatomy. One of the more vociferous ladies broke the momentary silence.

"Oh, you're right. They are pointed. That's a dead give away. Where are you from?"

"The Pleiades," was his unhesitating response.

"Yeah, I thought so. You know, ears are a good way, but I think eyes are the best way to tell. Some people have these large, almond eyes. You just know they're E.T.'s. . . ."

I leaned back and took a big swig, briefly wondering if this cosmic organization had a refund policy. It was going to be a long four days.

Another lady spoke up. "Head shape is also a way to tell. . . . Sabina, come here."

Hearing my friend's name, I spun around with hope. . . . Ah, someone to talk to and hopefully interpret for me.

"See, Sabina's eyes give her away."

Sabina smiled knowingly while greeting everyone at the table, lingering just a bit longer when our eyes met.

"Where are you from, Sabina?"

"I don't know," she said with a shrug. "Maybe the Pleiades."

"You know," one of the women continued, "it's just so obvious that E.T.'s have been living among us for centuries. You can see their inherited features everywhere. It's hard to understand why more people don't recognize that."

"Yeah, I'm glad we don't have to have pedigrees; we're all so mixed by now," the man interjected loudly.

As everyone finished chuckling, one of the women who hadn't said very much spoke up. "Has anyone been to the vortexes, yet?"

Everyone seemed to be nodding affirmatively except me and the woman who posed the question.

"Now, Bell Rock is distinctly masculine. . . very powerful," volunteered the man.

"That's true, but I find its energy a little harsh," came a response from the other side of the table. "I mean it's nice, but I much prefer Cathedral Rock. It seems to be just the right blend of masculine and feminine."

"Cathedral's okay, quite good in fact, but Boynton Canyon. . . . The energy there is so etheric and up-lifting. I feel like I'm ascending every time I meditate there."

"Well, for ascending energy, Airport Mesa Vortex is just so light and sweet. . . a very harmonious blend of feminine with the etheric. . . ."

I had the definite feeling I had gotten off the elevator on the wrong floor. Just then a shrill sound as loud as an air raid siren pierced my ears. As it finally lowered in intensity, another shriek joined in, not quite as loud, but in perfect harmony. Both sounds continued down the scale to about middle C where they abruptly and mercifully stopped. In the far corner of the living room sat a grinning 'Friar Tuck." Next to him in a matching swivel lounge chair sat a woman with long dark hair, gazing mysteriously at the rest of us. With joy and excitement pouring out of his robust posture, the rotund man began speaking in a high voice with a strong accent that I couldn't place.

"Well, how you all doin'?"

"Fine," came the chorus from almost everyone as they began scurrying for positions of vantage for whatever was about to happen.

I, too, moved closer, casually looking around in hopes of glimpsing the contraption that could have made those high pitched screeches to be sure I didn't end up sitting next to it. But, before I could navigate myself to an open spot against the far wall, the man and woman, now the undisputed center of attention, leaned back their heads and let out with another round of these piercing, sonic warbles. I paused in amazement. I couldn't believe vocal chords could make such sounds. Before I could look around to see if anyone else shared my reaction, most of the others began their own versions of "name that screech." I quickly settled into my corner to unobtrusively watch. The scene could roughly be compared to an orchestra warming up before the main performance, except these musicians had obviously misplaced their instruments and were trying unsuccessfully to imitate music with their own voices, and evidently believing the audience wouldn't notice. I cautiously allowed a tentative tone to come out of my own mouth, giving me just enough credibility to casually look around at my fellow virtuosos. At least half of them were now also waving their hands as if describing the swimming motion of frightened eels. Some, obviously accustomed to such performances, had quickly risen to their feet for maximum volume and attention. The cacophony finally crescendoed and then faded as the man and woman who had initiated it relaxed to just sit back and smile at everyone. I was face to face with Salizar and Solarra, the dubious, unearthly leaders of the seminar.

"The first thing we must do is release old patterns and allow our energy to flow," Salizar began. He was obviously overweight but, as he bounced on the edge of his chair while talking, his fluid movements and strength gave the impression of his being a dancer. "We have too much energy being used to maintain old patterns. Releasing this energy is necessary to balance the Chakras. Let the energy from the lower Chakras be released to come up into the higher Chakras. We'll work on our physical bodies first and then go to the emotional and the mental bodies. . . . I'm going to show you how to do adjustments on each other, then I want you all to do them until everyone has their energy flowing into the higher Chakras."

With that he asked one of the women in the front row to allow him to "adjust her," which she quickly agreed to. He directed her to stretch out on the floor while he knelt beside her, placing his right hand on her crotch and resting his left hand between her breasts. Then, opening his mouth like it contained a large egg, he emitted another series of uncivilized tones. This "adjustment" took about three or four minutes and was completed by his waving a hand in a haphazard fashion over her body. She laid there limp, obviously content and purring.

As he returned to his perch, he looked toward the rest of us. "Okay, these adjustments must be made by opposite charges in order to complete the circuit and balance the energy. This means men will adjust women, and women will adjust men. Men, your right hand on the first Chakra should point up, women, your right hand will point down. The left hand goes on the fourth Chakra over the heart. . . ."

I had already calculated that out of the eighteen of us there were only six men, including the leader. So, although this seminar had the prospect of being a long one, it appeared as if it would have its moments.

". . . . You guys are going to have to spread yourselves around to adjust all the women. . . . Okay, let's get going."

About half the people began stirring to pair up, but not me. There were several women whom I was immediately inclined to "adjust," but I didn't want to be obvious. After all, this was

a serious exercise with much more importance than to stimulate any adolescent fantasies that might happen to arise. I
think I did remarkably well in controlling my drooling, erotic
enthusiasm when one of my top three choices looked passed
the several swiveling heads between us and raised her eyebrows
to query me.

She wanted to adjust me first, which was fine. I needed to
think about what kind of inhuman noises I could possibly
make when it came my turn. As she put her hand on my "first
Chakra," I suddenly developed the morbid fear that this
adjustment process might cause an erection. Our leader had
neglected to mention how to handle such an emergency (if
indeed "handle" is the right word). Finally realizing that this
worry was probably more of a wish than reality, I relaxed
enough to enjoy the experience, although I wasn't exactly sure
what it was supposed to accomplish. Then I was the adjuster.
It felt strange to put my hands on this beautiful woman's
personal anatomy without having spent at least several weeks
of dating and plotting a strategy on how to maneuver her
consent to such an action. Here she was lying in a state of
enjoyment, or at least agreement, while my hands rested
firmly on her sexuality; and we didn't even know each other.
It felt somehow out of sequence.

I self-consciously made some acceptable sounds by singing
as high as my vocal chords would permit and then moving the
tone off key enough to sound original. After a few minutes I
lifted my hands a few inches above her body in a jerky fashion
and then sat back reasonably satisfied with my first completed
Chakra "adjustment." She opened her eyes after a few
seconds to smile and indicate that she had gotten a lot out of
the adjustment. I was not at all clear what I was doing, but,
with the ratio of men to women being what it was, I felt it was
incumbent on me to defer my own concerns in deference to the
needs of the group as a whole. It took two or three more such
efforts before I felt completely relaxed. Once I did, I actually
was able to get an impression of whether the adjustee's energy

was up or down, scattered or focused, intense or weak. Asking my partners immediately afterward allowed me to check out my impressions, which were more often right than not.

Everyone had been adjusted in about twenty minutes and, as Salizar brought the group together, the energy in the room was electric. He pointed that out before going on and everyone smiled, looking around in bright-eyed recognition. "This is a very special gathering. Each of you represent hundreds of thousands of beings from where you come from. . . ."

Boy, was he wrong about me. There's no more than six people, tops, back in San Francisco who even knew I was there. And, two of those didn't even care if I came back.

". . . . You are all from different star systems and are captains of space crafts that are right now hovering above the Earth. This is a council meeting of some extraordinary beings to help bring about heaven on Earth. . . ."

•　　　•　　　•

We were well into the third day before I had things pieced together. Salizar and Solarra were "walk-ins." That is, they used to be just regular people with regular names, John and Julie, I think, and had all the ups and downs of normal lives. They didn't even know each other. One day John was visited by an entity, called Avinon. Avinon told John that John's mission on Earth was complete and he, Avinon, would be taking over John's body as part of a project to bring about heaven on Earth. Understandably, this idea stretched John's sense of reality a bit; but after many animated discussions, John finally agreed. The switch was made and John returned to his residence in another dimension, where he still contributes to the overall project. Then, when Avinon met Akria (previously named Julie) there was an immediate recognition of their being partners in doing this work. All seemed to be going well until one night there came another tapping at the door. Two other entities, Salizar and Solarra, were ready to "walk-in" and begin their designated assignments in these human bodies. So Avinon and Akria held a ceremony to say good bye to their confused friends and to welcome in the new tenants. And, as any "new ager" might predict, they've been giving seminars ever since.

Their mission had two major components. Other extra-terrestrials were coming to Earth at this time to assist in the transformation of the planet from our current system of living together to one that works. These two walk-ins were to create a microcosm of this transformational process with their own lives that would serve to rally and support the numerous other walk-ins arriving daily. In addition, Salizar and Solarra were to put out a "wake-up" call to the multitude of extra-terrestrials who had been born here and simply remained asleep, those space travellers who had a part to play in Earth's transformation but were under the delusional belief of being just normal people.

Both Salizar and Solarra were able to channel transmissions from entities throughout the Universe; and, although I did not truly experience them or anyone else in the group as extra-terrestrials, not that I was sure what such an experience was like, I did feel the information they imparted about how to facilitate heaven on Earth was quite clear and profound. I also figured out the name game. Just about everyone in the group was convinced they were a "walk-in," and many had harrowing stories of near death experiences that directly preceded the knowledge, or apprehension, that they had just stepped into their bodies. To signify and help adjust to this revelation, the taking of new names such as Kosh-Kar or Altrinia was often adopted.

To confirm that I wasn't a walk-in or a wake-up, I kept reassuring myself that my being at this strange gathering was simply a coincidence; however, I half-way expected my inner "friend" to pipe up at any time and inform me that this seminar was it's humane way of gently letting me know my current lease had run out, and that I had thirty days to vacate this body.

I remained in this state of curious apprehension until the evening of the third day when Salizar abruptly began a process that unexpectedly changed everything.

·   ·   ·

"I'd like you all to think about the situations that you hate. What are the situations that drive you crazy? . . . That one thing that you absolutely cannot stand. . . ." He then sat back, signalling that we should take our time to be thorough.

I really didn't need a lot of time. The greatest pain I had ever experienced, and in a way was still experiencing, had come from the aborted relationship with Dawyn. So, for me, someone breaking their commitment of love was obviously the thing I hated the most. Knowing I had an answer, I sat back and relaxed, casually noticing that some of the others seemed to be going through quite a bit of internal dialogue, which puzzled me. What could be worse than someone offering love and then pulling it away, something everyone has undoubtedly experienced? But, just to be sure, I asked myself the question again.

A particular scene, which I had all but forgotten, came immediately to mind. It was a conversation with Dawyn after I had told her I was moving out of the house in Denver. I was packing things from my office area into boxes. I could hear Dawyn upstairs talking convivially on the phone to her friends as usual, which only annoyed and depressed me further. Feeling hopelessly alone, I sat back and just let my frustration come out in a stream of cathartic tears. Suddenly, Dawyn appeared in the doorway, having found something of mine on her desk that she assumed I would want to pack. I immediately turned away but, seeing my depression, she came to my side and asked if there were something she could do.

"Something you can do for me?" I screamed, but only to myself as I turned to look in her eyes. "Yeah, you can love me like you promised." But, as these unspoken thoughts raged in my mind, I realized she had a right not to love me the way I wanted her to. How and who we love is surely a divine right. Even though this hurt more than I cared to admit, I could accept it. What I simply could not accept was not knowing why.

"I can accept the fact that our love has changed," I stated resolutely. "But, I just need to understand why." Saying these words aloud brought more tears to my eyes and great embarrassment, as though I was somehow admitting a major character flaw and therefore was even more unlovable.

She stepped back and looked off into the imaginary distance as if hunting for a lost word. "You know, Rich. . . ." Her eyes found mine as she began and I could see her profound empathy for my plight, but she simply could not give to me what she did not have. At this point she appeared resigned to not knowing. ". . . . in life, understanding is the booby prize."

That was it! That was the moment, the instant, the epitome of what I hated. . . .

"Okay, has everybody got it?" Salizar refocussed everyone's attention with his energetic manner. "Okay, look at this situation, or situations, again and ask yourselves, 'What is the one thing here that I cannot compromise, the one thing that I must experience?'"

Shutting my eyes to go back to that traumatic moving day, I could see that Dawyn's love was what I thought I wanted most in the world, and having it taken away was devastating, but her right. Her response let me know that what I really wanted above all else was the truth, whatever that might be. What I perceived as her lack of concern for the truth I simply could not accept, and it had continued to fester an unequalled abhorrence within me ever since.

"If some of you don't get anything right now, that's okay. For those who do, just know that it is an indicator of your Essence, also known as Spirit. . . . Your Essence is the unique vibration or frequency of consciousness with which each of you are born, or with which each of you have come to Earth. It is the music of your soul, and its melody is unique in all the Universe. When you allow this Essence to be present in your actions, no matter what you are doing, you feel fulfilled, at peace, and on purpose. When this quality is blocked and not allowed to be expressed in your life, you intuitively feel something vital is missing."

I felt more than comfortable with the notion of having a unique vibration beneath all the trappings of my identity, and I reasoned that mine must have something to do with the discovery of truth, although of that I was not at all clear.

"My Essence is wisdom," Salizar continued. "When I am sharing it, I am totally alive and experience fulfillment. I can't stand to be in situations where wisdom is not honored or shared. So, those situations in your life that trigger an immense discomfort are usually the antithesis of your Essence. Such situations are clues that can help you discover the unique nature of your being—your Essence. Look at your life now in total, and see if there is any pattern in which you have experienced this extreme discomfort. . . ."

I saw a trend in my life of being ever-restless in my various jobs to the point of hating their empty monetary reward of success. I always abhorred party situations where there would be small talk that just seemed to ignore what life was all about. I fought the draft not so much as a political battle but as a personal war, because it simply was not what I was here to do—it was not the purpose of my life. I could see that with every romantic partner I was constantly sensing the relationship was meant to be something more, and, therefore, I blindly pushed to discover what that was. And my current quest of self-discovery was totally dedicated to this pursuit of truth.

"Think back again. . . . In these situations how did you feel about yourself?"

I never really felt very good about myself and my life,

maybe because most of my friends and family continually expressed concern about not understanding me, why I could never settle down, build a career, concentrate on a family, be content. In general, I always felt a little guilty and out of sync with the system and not being able to go along with the program. "Why can't I fit in? What will it take to make me happy?" I always seemed to attain a certain amount of outward success in my various endeavors but never any lasting satisfaction or fulfillment, which remained, even now, a perplexing source of self-recrimination and foreboding.

"Consider the possibility," Solarra, her angelic expression still conveying a bliss-like trance, softly spoke for the first time in a very deliberate, underscored tone that riveted everyone's attention. ". . . . that the very things you have thought were wrong with your life are, in truth, what's right about your life. . . . Whenever you felt deep discontent and confusion, it was simply your Essence refusing to surrender to a life where it could not be fully expressed. . . . Those situations are really blessings in disguise; and your frustrations, which may feel like weakness on your part, are, in truth, your greatest strength. . . ."

Gigantic tumblers began slipping into place, and a rusty vault door swung open to allow light in for the first time. There was no physical evidence or logic to support the notion that everyone is a unique Essence or Spirit; but somehow I knew it was true, and I realized I'd always known that truth at some level. What a joy to know that my Essence, though unseen, had been strong enough to endure all my years of going in circles. So that's what my internal "friend" was referring to when saying I'm at an extraordinary place in my life. Suddenly, my previous confusion and pain began to seem like less of a curse, as these ideas surrounded me like a soft familiar blanket.

"If you are one," she continued, "who can glimpse the flickering light of your Essence behind your demanding, daily desires, or can hear its whispers above your temporary thoughts, then you are indeed here with a purpose that cannot be denied."

I felt a burning desire to know exactly what my Essence was; and, as I looked around the room, I could see that I was not alone in this desire. We all began sharing our guesses in an excited fashion, qualities like Harmony, Abundance, Joy, Freedom of Expression, Playfulness, Inner Peace, Love, and Wisdom. Some felt sure of their first impression and others, like myself, could only narrow it down to a general area.

"Now, I want you to picture those situations in your life when you feel most alive. . . . Those situations when everything just seems to fall into place, when you can do no wrong, where you feel totally connected and purposeful. . . . What exactly are you doing? . . . Are you with people or alone? . . . How are you expressing yourself?"

There was instant recognition here also—it was obviously those times when I was in a process of self-discovery, or when I was in situations where others were discovering their truths.

"These situations will give you some idea of your purpose and the particular method in which it is natural for you to express your Essence. For instance, if your Essence is compassion and you love to sing, then your purpose is to express compassion through song. When you do, everyone hearing this expression of your Essence will have the opportunity to be a little more awakened to their own Essence. . . . You can see how the awareness of your Essence and purpose can greatly simplify life. Making decisions becomes a relatively easy matter—just take the path that allows for the greatest expression of Essence and is aligned with your purpose. . . ."

It wasn't Sedona, or their house, or even the people there, though all of that was nice; but for the first time in my life I felt I was home—home within myself. I was acknowledging and beginning to fully experience a connection with the "me" behind all the stuff I acted like. Although it was still hard to clearly distinguish, I had the certainty of consciously touching my own unique flame of life for the first time ever.

•   •   •

On the last session of the last day, Salizar was summing up by sharing a twelve part process for manifesting visions. At one point, while the room was very quiet as we all pondered and made notes of a particularly important step, I noticed a hawk circling outside the window. Excitedly, I began to point at it and may have even said, "Look," but was swiftly stopped by Salizar who, without even glancing out the window, quickly held up his hand to arrest my intention and said, "It is for you." The whole incident happened so fast, maybe only one or two others even noticed. For several minutes, I sat back and watched the hawk until it soared from view before returning my attention to the room.

The seminar ended later that day, and it was with mixed emotions that I prepared to leave these "visitors" from outer space. Sabina and I had realized we were just friends, which was just as well with all the thoughts going through my mind. Even though much of what I saw and heard over the four days was far beyond my threshold of plausibility, I had undeniably experienced a remarkable connection with my Essence and somehow knew my life would never be the same, which was, if nothing else, a relief. I had not been even remotely inclined to see myself as an extra-terrestrial "walk-in," a reluctance to which Salizar and Solarra readily agreed because they were convinced I was really a "wake-up!" In gratitude for what I had received, I did not try to dissuade them from this folly. It seemed a relatively minor point and, since there was an air of romantic intrigue to such a notion, I merely indicated I would take it under advisement.

I said my good-byes to these loving beings and, by late afternoon, I was on the road, eager to discover even more of my Essence when home. I had planned to drive up to Winslow to see the meteorite crater but, once behind the wheel, changed my mind, preferring to let my thoughts wander on the less-used backroads of Arizona as opposed to cruising on the busy freeway. After just a few minutes on this one particular route, I saw something fluttering off to the side, but was well passed it by the time I could stop. I ran back, observing now that it was a hawk. The flutter of its wing had obviously been initiated by a breeze, for the once majestic bird was dead, maybe an hour or two; its head bloodied by some violent act. I had always wanted to have some hawk feathers but never imagined I would find them still attached to their owner. As I lifted its deceptively light body in my hands, I felt a distinct reverence for this magnificent creature. In addition, I had the unmistakable knowledge of what I must do, as if I had done it many times before.

I carried it away from the road and located a spot under the tallest tree-like shrub in the area. Using sticks, I dug at the rock-strewn ground for quite awhile, until I had a hole big enough for a grave. A short meditation seemed in order, but as I shut my eyes a distant chant started coming out of my mouth. It was a plaintive native American sound worthy of many drums. I silently asked the hawk if I could take its wings and immediately got the impression that I could if I left something I valued in their place. With my small pocket knife, a gift from a dear friend years before, I cut the wings free. A small amount of muscle and sinew hung precariously from one of the wings and, overcoming an immediate revulsion that stiffened my body, I intuitively knew I must taste it as part of this impromptu but ancient ritual. I then asked if I could take the talons and had the definite feeling not to. I placed my knife on the hawk's body and covered both with dirt, resuming my chant for a few more minutes before leaving.

The sun was slipping from view and streaking the evening sky with pastels as I returned to my truck. I eased behind the wheel and carefully placed the freed wings in my daypack on the passenger's seat. As I started to pull back onto the road, a large owl came into view off to my left, about fifty feet away and heading straight toward me at a very high rate of speed. When just ten feet from my open window, it flipped its tail feathers down, swinging its large body vertical and momentarily exposing the entire underside of its beautiful white wings. This maneuver shot it straight up into the twilight and out of sight. I probably said "wow" or something to that effect, and then recalled the other owl I had seen on the trip out. I had to smile, considering myself lucky to be chancing upon so many unusual encounters. Then, like a brilliant shooting star, Savizar's earlier statement silently snared my awareness—"It is for you."

A cold spasm ran down my spine. Could Salizar have meant those words literally? Could the hawk I'd found have been the same one circling outside the seminar? But, I didn't even know I was going to be on this particular road. It was a last second decision, or was it?"

I let the truck roll to a slow stop to the side of the road and got out to walk around. It was a warm night, inviting me to sit against a nearby manzanita clump and look at the stars while I considered the strange events of the last few days. . . .

"What does all this mean?" I asked out-loud of my internal "friend" to finally break the silence.

"Could only mean one thing. . . . You've finally earned your 'wings' from the Universe."

I acted annoyed. "You just can't pass up a pun, can you?"

"Sorry," it replied with a devilish inflection.

"Can we get serious, now?"

"Sure."

"What do these weird events have to do with my Essence?"

"What gives the hawk it's great power to soar into the sky?"

Its immediate reply, like abruptly shifting gears, caught me off guard. I scrunched my face a little as the obvious answer slowly appeared. "Its wings," I tentatively ventured.

"The hawk does need strong wings to realize it's destiny, but they are not what gives the hawk it's power. It is the invisible wind that surrounds its wings that lifts the hawk to it's greatness."

I pictured that in my mind and smiled at its truth.

"And so it is with you."

I paused. "What do you mean?"

"You take pride in your mind and its ability to comprehend and create the beliefs of your identity. You think that your mind will lift you to your destiny and enable you to find your love and destiny."

I stared off into the distance while I looked inside.

"It is true that you need a strong mind for the journey, but it is your Essence, the invisible Spirit that surrounds your mind, which will lift you to your greatness."

I took a deep breath, not knowing what to say. "Have you known all along about my Essence?"

"Of course."

"Why haven't you talked to me about it?"

"You can't begin to see or experience your Essence until you are ready, until you have reached that place on your journey."

I wondered how much time I had wasted. "Can you tell me more about it now?"

"Everyone's Essence (Spirit) is a little different, like a particular melody or a specific color. What would you like to know?"

"Well, Salizar knows his Essence to be that of wisdom. And some of the others in the group were sure of theirs, like compassion and inner peace. I know mine has something to do with truth and self-discovery but. . . ."

"Wanting to categorize it with a single word is something only the mind desires in its effort to comprehend it; but your Essence, like consciousness itself, is beyond mental comprehension. All you need to do is follow your intuition and you will naturally experience and express your Essence more and more in your daily life, continually refining your knowledge of it."

"Well, how can I know when I'm hearing my intuition or whether it's one of the voices from my identity?"

"That's easy. Intuition always invites rather than pushes because it has infinite patience, knowing that everything you do leads to further self-discovery. . . . In addition, your intuition never makes choices based on whether others will like it or not, for it marches to the rhythm of your Essence. . . . And you can hear that unique sound whenever you want just by shutting your eyes and listening to your heart. This is how you can tell it from any other voice you hear. . . ."

I stayed in that extraordinary peaceful state for quite some time before finally opening my eyes, stretching, and resuming the long drive back to the Bay Area.

•   •   •

Upon arriving home to collect my mail and messages, I considered myself doubly fortunate to have spent that previous week in Arizona. If I'd remained in California undoubtedly I would have caught the powerfully contagious flu bug that had mysteriously afflicted every single one of the second group of manuscript readers, preventing each from perusing much past the introduction. And, with all those I could reach, my heart was touched by their unselfish suggestions of letting someone else have this previewing honor while they recuperated. Naturally, I declined these gracious and often vehement offers of self-sacrifice, assuring them of my uncommon patience. However, since I did not have a reviewed manuscript to occupy my time as anticipated, I welcomed this as further opportunity to explore the inner doors opened in Sedona. Maybe my "friend" could suggest ways in which I might discover more of my Essence and its connection with the Universe.

"Go dancing," came its swift reply.

.   .   .

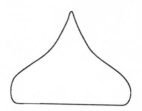

The frame is fastened, the canvass stretched,
And an image drawn of someone else,
Then subtle shades brushed and colors sketched,
But, in truth, we always paint our Self.

Chapter Twelve

(**The Explorer**, Warrior, Wanderer, Magician)

The Portrait of Power

"Go dancing!?" I repeated incredulously.

Such a quick and off-the-wall response convinced me that I must not have enunciated my question correctly. Not only did this bizarre suggestion seem inappropriate, I didn't even like dancing. Well, it wasn't that I didn't like it as much as I usually felt a little awkward doing it, especially without a date. Given these factors, it didn't seem too unreasonable to ask the question a second time for clarification, which of course produced the identical response. The unusual name of a dance club, The Barefoot Boogie, appeared in my memory from some idle past conversation, and I slowly gathered the necessary clothes and courage to comply. After all, it couldn't be worse than hot coals, could it?

The club sported a modern motif with a friendly atmosphere and contained no less than three dance floors with all the latest in electronic lighting. Finding a seat near the end of the long ornate bar, I spent my first two bottles of mineral water trying to decide who in the large crowd to inflict myself upon, since I assumed the directive that got me there did not intend for me to flitter around solo. My heart was still not fully into this decision but, finally accepting that fact, I just relaxed to watch the dozen or so dancers within my view interpret the rock music while flashing strobes turned their fluid movements into robotic motion.

Though everything was pretty much what I expected, within a few minutes I sensed something behind the scenes that I hadn't been conscious of before. A Johnny Mathis song started playing and several couples began doing the basic slow-dance box step. However it didn't take more than a few seconds of casual scrutiny to realize that each pair was dancing in their own distinct style. Looking around the bar, I could see that no one was drinking in exactly the same way, either. I even noticed that I seemed to be the only one letting a few little pieces of ice slip through with each sip so that I could crunch them with my teeth. As I continued glancing around, I graphically saw that all of us were essentially doing the same things in life, yet we each did them in very unique ways. Every single thought, feeling, action, and sensation was the result of a kind of partnership with the Universe. We were all somehow given the energy of life but how we used it, how we transformed that energy into the peculiar style of our lives, was unique to each of us.

This idea was strangely comforting. I pictured my own, convoluted life as a stretched canvas with each of my thoughts being a design, each feeling a color, and every action a brush stroke. Even though the painting seemed to be thoroughly impressionistic and understood by none, not even me, it was consoling to realize that I was the painter. Obviously, I could go back and redo it the way I wanted, that is once I was finished with this quest, once I fully understood my Essence and life's purpose. . . . But, something about that thought stopped me. I was doing it again—I was waiting. I had said stuff like that to myself a million times. "As soon as I find my soulmate, then I'll be happy. As soon as I understand life, then I can begin to fulfill my destiny and do some really important things in this world." Suddenly seized with the realization that this unique co-creative partnership with the Universe was right there in the moment, I sat my nearly empty glass down, stood up, and strode toward the attractive and animated brunette I had noticed earlier sitting in a group a few bar stools down.

Possibly spurred by the same realization, it appeared this bright-eyed beauty was in the process of standing up to greet me as I arrived. Before any words were spoken I took her hand and led us onto the hardwood floor where we began gyrating under the pulsing strobes, periodically letting our smiles mingle. The music, as well as persistent thoughts, poured through me, and I shut my eyes to muse over my current insights. I had been living my life never really looking at or acknowledging this co-creative partnership with the Universe. "How could this have happened?" I said out loud forgetting where I was.

"What do you mean. Weren't you going to ask me to dance?" My pretty partner slowed down enough to look me directly in my now open eyes as she queried in response to my absentminded rhetoric.

I chuckled, realizing the obvious misinterpretation and sought to reassure her by casually explaining that I was just talking to myself. I planned, of course, to share with her the entire sequence of profound thought that led up to the misunderstood comment, as well as some of the more interesting aspects of my life story; but for some reason she quickly returned to the safety of her friends as the song ended. It didn't matter though. I had found what I came for and left to walk in the night air.

People were free to use this energy from the Universe to co-create any type of life they wanted, but why were there so many apparent inequities? Two people could have roughly the same kind of life-style and one would be happy, the other miserable. Or two people could have very different morals, one being very ruthless and self-centered and the other being kind and generous, yet the ruthless person could become much more prosperous than the kind one. In fact, that seemed to happen more often than not. I wondered if there were specific rules that governed this co-creative partnership, and, if so, how did they allow for such variety of disparate lives?

•   •   •

Over the next couple months, as time permitted, I voraciously read everything I could find even remotely related to this idea of a co-creative partnership with the Universe. My focus narrowed down to the methods of "visualization" and "affirmation." Because the only criterion for using them was to be alive, I felt sure these were the designated tools of this co-creative partnership.

The basic premiss of these techniques is simply to visualize what you want to have happen, make affirmative statements out-loud that fully support that event occurring, and then live your life with the confidence that it will. According to the theory, pretty soon it will.

The first thing I did was look back at my life and see if I had ever, even if unknowingly, used successfully visualizations or affirmations successfully, thereby validating their credibility. I recalled times when I had pictured particular jobs that I had wanted and, sure enough, ended up in that occupation. I also recalled times when I had been discouraged and unsure about something only to somehow get through it by affirming to myself that I would. But, for every memory that supported these theories, there seemed to be an inconclusive or non-supportive one. The only sure way to discover if these techniques would allow me to actively co-create my life was to perform my own controlled experiment. I would simply decide on something that I wanted to have happen, visualize and affirm it according to the prescribed methods of the experts, and give it a reasonable time to happen.

Isolating myself in my apartment, I shut my eyes and asked myself what I currently desired most and (surprise) immediately pictured myself in bed with a beautiful woman. "Now, this is my kind of experiment," I said for some objective encouragement. But, then I reasoned that such a request might not be a fair test for this co-creative partnership with the Universe. If the past was any indication, engineering such a situation could take a long time, painfully longer than

I wanted to contemplate. However, who said life was fair? Besides, if I made my goal too easy, I would probably just rationalize away the results as coincidence. So, in the interest of science, I spent at least a half hour dutifully going through the visualization and affirmation processes recommended to achieve the desired romantic situation and, again being objective, requested that it occur within the next twenty-four hours.

As with other well-meaning intentions, within a few hours I had forgotten all about this project and was hurriedly going through the day's scheduled events, one of which was to make a necessary, brief appearance at a friend's birthday party. Allowing myself about ten minutes for this commitment, I hurriedly bounced into Millie's, a noisy vegetarian restaurant in San Rafael, and quickly located the celebration table. I was casually introduced by the guest of honor to a few new faces in the group, one of which belonged to a woman whose coy but inviting smile provided more than enough incentive to totally ignore the several penciled-in appointments remaining on my insistent calendar. Now, it just so happened that I did end up spending the night with her, but I'm not totally sure that it validates the afore-mentioned affirmation and visualization hypothesis because the interaction between us, though technically conforming to my request, fell far short of living up to my expectations.

As we shared a pasta salad during dinner and it became apparent that a romantic opportunity was emerging, certain priorities clicked in that completely dominated my thoughts. Although she was extremely attractive and I very much wanted to make love to her, I really didn't know her as anything other than a friend of a friend. Being a believer in safe sex, there were some preliminaries to delicately discuss before that could happen, like had she been tested for AIDS lately? Did she need to be tested? How did she feel about condoms, and did she happen to have one with her? Since the answers to these questions seemed eminently more time-critical than the overall experiment, I abandoned my mental lab coat and clip-board all together. About three hours later we were (as they say) alone and prone, and I was deftly maneuvering the conversation toward the desired information when she made a declaration that immediately reduced the urgency of my immediate health concerns.

"I have five lovers right now, and I guess I could take on a sixth; but anyone who would be my lover must first sign a 'social marriage contract' with me."

Thinking this a clever put-on, I began a short-lived laugh. Here we were, snuggled together in a warm sleeping bag, our naked bodies touching, all the sounds and aromas of approaching intimacy present, and suddenly there was the incongruent rustling of a two page legal document materializing between us and a monotone recitation of its contents, not unlike a lawyer reading a will. She was not joking; and, although curious as to what could comprise such a social contract, I was stunned to silence.

"These first two points are non-negotiable. If you can't agree to them, there's no way we can be involved. First, you agree to work toward a live-in group marriage comprised of two men and two women. The four of us will be married to each other but each can have selective relationships outside of the marriage. Second, you agree to strive for physical immortality."

"Oh, my God, a 'Rebirther'!" I thought to myself, "and that wasn't one of the disciplines I studied."

". . . . Shall I go on?" she asked rather routinely.

I merely nodded my head. Words would have been superfluous.

"You agree to be affectionate every day, practicing "sexual Kung Fu" when possible. . . ."

I, of course, acted like I knew what that was, not wanting

to seem naive in these matters and rationalizing that in meeting the first two conditions I would have plenty of time and opportunity to learn this intriguing third condition, undoubtedly some rare martial arts discipline developed to combat industrial strength diaphragms.

". . . . You agree to share your feelings. . . ."

The remaining seventeen stipulations were enough within the range of normalcy that I was able to tune her out in hopes of formulating a sophisticated response by the time she finished. However, I probably would have needed a week or so of intense reflection to manage anything more than a smile, which is all I offered as she concluded and looked up expectantly.

She must have interpreted this gesture as a tentative agreement to her conditions because she gleefully put the contract away and nestled closer, saying "Now, there is something you should know before we get started. . . ."

Something more? I couldn't imagine.

"I do have herpes, but it's under control. Whenever I get an outbreak I take this organic medicine and it goes away pretty quickly. But, I don't have it right now, so I think we're safe. . . ."

Well, there was a load off my mind. . . . It did occur to me that possibly I could paint my picture of the ideal, monogamous relationship in such an intriguing way as to entice this beautiful woman into considering something a little less adventurous than her current ambitions; but before I could formulate such words, if indeed they existed, she proceeded to describe for me a small community she was considering joining in lieu of finding the ideal foursome.

"They live in the large house in San Francisco, about thirty-five people I'd guess, a few more men than women. But, they're a little too regimented for me."

That was somewhat hard to believe.

"They subscribe to 'poly-fidelity.' It works this way. If you want to join the community and you're accepted, you stay celibate for four months while everyone gets to know everyone. Then, whichever family. . . . Oh, the thirty-five people are divided into four or five families, I think, and each family has about five of six people in it. So, whichever small group feels aligned with you takes you into their family. They then practice group poly-fidelity. . . ."

I imagined this could be one solution to the homeless problem.

"But, I don't really like how they decide who sleeps with whom. They have a weekly chart that rotates each of the family members so that they switch partners every night. That means if there's an odd number in the family group, you'll end up sleeping alone some nights. Of course, you don't have to sleep with someone you're assigned to if you don't want to or if you have a cold or something. . . ."

Very civilized of them—sort of a collaboration between the Rhahsnesh and George Orwell. It was definitely time to tell her the marginally bad news that a social marriage with three other people was just not what I was looking for. I had always seen myself in a relationship with just one other person. Maybe group marriages were the "families" of the future but it didn't feel right for me, although I really couldn't say why. Certainly my serial monogamy had not yet proven to be an overwhelmingly successful vehicle on my path to happiness. However, I knew how unhappy I had been over the failure of my more traditional marriages. I didn't even want to think of how depressing it would be to fail at a marriage with three people simultaneously. However, here I was confronted with another situation that challenged by beliefs about there being one special person with whom to share love and through whom I would find my destiny. Was I missing the message here?

Realizing this relationship had peaked, I asked if she thought she'd be successful in eventually creating this group marriage, especially since she'd been trying unsuccessfully now for several years. There was more than just a hint of doubt in her quick, affirmative answer, which may be why she felt compelled to defend her philosophy by explaining that dolphins embody promiscuity with a superior level of intelligence. Well, I knew there was evidence to suggest that dolphins did have a high level of intelligence, maybe even consciousness, along with ample proof that their complex social behavior included a variety of sexual behavior. However, I was not aware of any evidence to suggest that practicing the latter would produce the former. In the interest of logic I felt obliged to point out that dolphins in the wild also eat nothing but live, raw fish and that maybe this activity, rather than their sexual patterns, was the real contributing factor to their level of intelligence or consciousness. She must have mistaken this insightful offering as sarcasm, because it was at this point that she unceremoniously rolled over and began to go to sleep.

Strangely enough, it was also about that this time my scientific dedication returned, and I realized I was actually in bed with a woman loosely complying with the specifications of my recent affirmation and visualization. The experiment had been a success in that I had roughly co-created what I set out to by using those techniques; however I still didn't feel any closer to understanding how this co-creative partnership with the Universe worked, a perplexion I resolved to discuss with my "friend" at the first available opportunity.

•   •   •

Once again in the security of my own apartment and without the pleasant distraction of a naked woman lying next to me, I optimistically thought I'd get right to the point. "Is there a Universal Law that governs our ability to co-create our lives?"

"Yes," came the usual reassuring tone and quick response.

"What is it?"

"Which part?"

Why did I think this conversation was going to be any easier than the others? I took a deep breath. "Okay, the part that allows me to manifest things in my life through visualizations and affirmations."

"Attraction."

"That's it. One word—attraction?"

"You say you like to figure things out on your own when you can."

"Well, that's true, I do. But, I've tried on this one. . . and that's why I'm talking to you, I mean talking to myself like an idiot."

"Try again."

Reluctantly, I shut my eyes and began to try to analyze what I had just heard. I was able to manifest things by attracting them. Within a minute or two, my attempts at logic began to slip away, and an incident came to mind that had occurred when I was a probation officer, years before. Several of us in the department had been offered a chance to try out a bio-feedback machine, a real fad for a year or two in the 70's. I remembered the device being put on my head that could measure the four separate brain waves emitted by either side of my brain. Each brain wave—alpha, beta, delta, or theta—when present, would elicit a specific tone. By concentrating on a particular set of tones, I was able to control my brain waves. Remembering this scene, I realized that for the machine to pick up these signals they had to somehow exit my body. From this I could mentally see that my entire body was a continuous stream of electro-chemical reactions that created electrical and magnetic currents, which could actually be collected and measured by sensors placed close to me. This meant that my thoughts and feelings and any activity in my physical body were immediately converted to impulses that created a electro-magnetic field around my body. And this strange but discernible field would obviously be unique to me as it contained the electro-magnetic patterns of everything going on inside of me.

"So there's actually a physical manifestation of this rule of attraction. A person's magnetic field or aura contains the imprint of whatever is being thought and felt. This unique energy signature is what attracts whatever is desired."

"See, you knew all along."

"Yeah, but tell me this. I did end up sleeping with a beautiful woman, which is, in general, what I visualized; but it wasn't at all what I really expected. Why wasn't she more like me and possibly even a candidate for being that special person? Does the Universe sometimes misread electro-magnetic fields?"

"Nothing is ever provided to you by the Universe unless there is a indicator of your fascination with it. The Universe picks up everything you put out magnetically, whether you are aware of it or not. "

"But. . . ." I stopped myself to grasp the full, dreadful impact of this notion. This meant that unless I was totally conscious of all my desires and thoughts I wouldn't even know what I was attracting into my life. It also meant that if my life was in painful havoc, it wasn't a result of anything Dawyn did, nor was it because the Universe's rules of co-creation were inconsistent. If my life wasn't the way I wanted, it was because I wasn't putting out clear signals; I was responsible! "Okay, but it is possible that the Universe might make a little mistake now and then. I mean it might think it's picking up a signal that I want something when I really don't, right?"

"There is a guiding set of Universal Laws* from which the Universe never varies."

*For more the complete set of Universal Laws, see Appendix.

"Then what you're telling me is that everything that comes into my life is being attracted by what I'm thinking, feeling, and doing?"

"Anything in your life to which you react—yes! That's one of the beauties of the partnership. If you're ever unclear about who you are, all you have to do is look around at the situations and people in your life. Collectively, they are a complete reflection of what's going on inside you."

"You mean each thing in my life is reflecting back to me that aspect of myself that attracted it? How can that be? Okay, I admit I consciously attracted this woman into my life within the allotted twenty-four hours, so I know the Universe can work that way. But, I wasn't putting out any signals to attract someone who wanted a group marriage. That was a real turn off to me."

"Maybe it would help to view it another way. Let's say that all your thoughts and feelings are translated into your magnetic field as tiny little holographic pictures. As soon as the Universe sees one of these little holograms, it begins arranging itself to provide you the opportunity of experiencing the reality of that picture. Does that seem reasonable?"

"Yeah." I hate it when I'm being led down a path that invariably circumvents my logic, especially when I can't see it until it happens.

"You say you don't have a desire for a group marriage so there shouldn't be a picture of that in your magnetic field, but you do have desires of having a monogamous relationship, especially a soulmated one, right?"

"Yeah."

"Well, behind every desire is attached some fear, fear that you won't get what you desire or fear that if you do you won't be able to keep it. These fears also create magnetic pictures. Since the Universe perceives your entire collection of pictures, it immediately begins arranging situations for you to experience all of them."

"But any magnetic images created from my fears are not pictures that I want to have materialize. It's the ones created from my desires that I want to experience."

"The Universe assumes that any picture you put in your magnetic field is something with which you are fascinated and therefore want to experience, otherwise why would you create it? And, the images that have the strongest and clearest signals get the greatest attention."

"So this woman was providing me with the opportunity to experience my fears about being in a non-monogamous relationship?"

"Do you have such fears?"

"Well, maybe. . . . Yeah, I guess so."

"Are they strong ones?"

"Okay, okay."

"This is why you have perceived people whom you consider to be of questionable ethics often prospering while others of great character, in your eyes, struggle to make a living. Everyone who uses the Universal Laws correctly can co-create anything they desire. The Universe does not make judgments as to who is worthy of this partnership and who is not."

"So I can use this co-creative partnership to make a million bucks if I want?"

"Sure."

"I don't have to be a partner with the Universe in any altruistic or purposeful way other than to co-create my desires?"

"Absolutely. People do it all the time—at least they try to."

"Ah, there it is. There's the fine print. You mean people can try, but they really can't misuse this co-creative process for selfish motives?"

"This partnership is often misused, not necessarily because of selfish intent, but because people don't really understand the way it works. For instance, if you have a belief that you are someone who could or should make a million dollars, the associated thoughts and emotions of that belief will generate a picture of you having a million dollars. This picture gets fed into your magnetic field and picked up as an image of your desire. The Universe will then begin arranging itself to provide you with that experience. It's automatic."

"Then why am I not a millionaire? Why isn't everyone?"

"Because, for every picture of happiness you have, you also have a picture of fear; they're the opposite and inseparable sides of the same coin. The Universe then arranges itself to provide you with these experiences, which are often the fearful ones because fears are usually stronger than desires. Consequently, life may seem very confusing and unpredictable. Is any of this familiar?"

I decided that any response to that last question would just encourage more such flippant remarks. "Well, now that I know how it works, what's to keep me from using it selfishly and making that million bucks, if I want to?"

"Nothing. . . . Nothing except yourself."

"You mean my conscience? . . . That I'd feel guilty?"

"Not exactly. The way to make a million bucks is to have all your thoughts, emotions, and actions directed toward that desire. In this way you will flood your magnetic field with the appropriate signals. The Universe will respond accordingly, and you'll soon have your million dollars."

"So, I'll screw up this process if I have any fears that get in the way."

"Right. And when living in an identity-based reality, it's impossible to have desires without at least some fear being attached to them. However, there are techniques, such as affirmations and visualizations, that can minimize these fears and help to strengthen the signal of the top one or two most desired pictures."

"But, it is possible, then. If I minimize my fears and establish a fifty-thousand-watt signal of that desire, I will make that million bucks, right?"

"Right. . . unless. . . ."

"I knew it. It's not guaranteed, is it? Unless what?"

"Think of the people you know who desire to make a million bucks and are doing it. The more successful ones are probably eating, sleeping, and breathing that desire. All of their thoughts, emotions and actions revolve around it, and the Universe is responding. To achieve it they cannot afford to entertain doubts, or other desires of any consequence, or any experiences of themselves that do not align with this desire."

"I could do that."

"Maybe you could, but the question is, 'will you?' Recently you have begun to experience your Essence and your life's purpose. You may find that the magnetic pictures generated by your Essence may not be as concerned with making a million bucks as the signals from your identity."

"So, if I want a million bucks I've got to sacrifice my Essence?"

"Not necessarily. It may be part of your Essence and purpose to co-create with the Universe even more than a million dollars, and it may not."

"This is discouraging. From what I know of it so far, I don't think my Essence cares whether it gets a million bucks or not."

"Such is often the nature of Essence. There is one consolation, though."

"What's that?"

"There's no amount of money that can buy the experience of Essence, nor the fulfillment derived when expressing it. That can only be had by taking the Spirit's Journey, which you have chosen."

I surprised myself on how persistent I had been about the million dollars. I knew my desire for money was part of a larger collection of fantasies that I kept in an inconspicuous mental tote bag in hopes that it would somehow get through spiritual customs when I landed at enlightenment. "So, I have an identity-based set of magnetic signals, and I have another emerging set that is based on experiencing life through my Essence. . . ."

"Right."

"And I can use my partnership with the Universe to co-create either. The Universe doesn't care which I do, right?"

"The Universal Laws and principles work for either reality."

"Pretty clever."

"This particular Principle of Attraction also provides the explanation for how Karma operates in your life."

It didn't take much to see the connection. "Whatever I do to others creates pictures in my magnetic field, and the Universe then arranges itself to let me experience those things myself. So, in essence they comes back to me."

"Bingo."

I just sat there for awhile, knowing "intuitively" the truth of these words. But the longer I pondered what had been said, the more I got the feeling something was missing. Essentially, we had covered the two fundamental ways life can be lived, through Essence or identity, and in all that discussion the idea of "love" hadn't been mentioned. In fact I hadn't even considered it until this moment, and I exited my pensive silence with that curiosity. . . .

"So, what's love got to do with it?"

In completing the journey we face all our fears,
Exacting their price for the truths we receive, .
And to reach that place where love appears,
We must first let go of all we believe.

Chapter Thirteen

The Price of Love

"To know what love has to do with co-creating your life, you must first know what love is. . . ."

My "friend" was obviously waiting for me to say something profound from my extensive understanding of the topic. After all, if sex can be included as a subcategory, love has been by far the most dominant preoccupation ever since my voice changed. However, I chose a more diplomatic response. "Well, I'm not sure it can be put into words."

"Maybe if you pictured the time you were most in love it would define itself?"

That thought immediately brought Dawyn's smile to mind. "Okay. Love is the strongest emotion that can be generated within me, and it occurs when I find someone or something who touches my being in such a way as to make my heart sing."

"That's pretty good, and I'm sure most people would accept that as a pretty fair description of their experience with love. But, unfortunately that's not love."

Obviously I needed to build from the ground up. "Love is the strongest emotion my heart can generate."

"Nope."

"Love is the strongest emotion in me."

"Sorry."

"Love is an emotion."

"I'm afraid you're getting colder."

"How can you say love is not an emotion? I feel it." I stood up abruptly, ostensibly to stretch my legs from sitting so long.

"You really can't see what love is until you first look at what you think it is and how you came to those beliefs. For instance, you defined yourself as good looking, therefore your partner would have to be pretty. You also saw yourself as active, witty, deserving of love, etc., so you looked for an active, witty Laura Petrie, who, of course, loved you passionately. Love, then, became the attraction you felt toward someone who happened to meet this criteria."

I began pacing and acting like I needed to go to the bathroom. Whenever these conversations got onto the subject of my identity, they usually ended up with painful revelations.

"Two things occurred with Dawyn that intensified this attraction. First, because of unsuccessful past relationships, you had released some of your more excessive criteria by the time you met her. And second, she appeared to match your remaining criteria much more than any previous candidate. But, what you felt was not love."

I plopped back down, intrigued but a little resentful. I knew that what I felt for Dawyn was love, at least I was sure it was the closest I'd ever been to it. But, if that wasn't love, what would a true experience of love be like? And could I live through it? "So, what I felt for her was what, infatuation?" I replied as a caustic challenge.

"You loved her as much as you could given all the conditions and criteria of your identity's beliefs."

"But, if I didn't have those conditions, how would I know my soulmate? How would I know who to love?"

"If you didn't have those conditions, how would you know who not to love?"

(Ouch) 'So, you're saying that everyone is worth loving; and, if I dropped my identity's conditions on who I should love, I would love everyone. . . . . Okay, in a way I know that, but I don't want to love everyone the way I love a special someone. Are you saying that free love or open marriages are the relationships of the future?"

"Just because you experience love with someone doesn't mean you have to express that love in any particular form. This is a common area of confusion because in an identity-based reality often one of the conditions of love is that it be expressed sexually."

I decided this was getting a little too close for comfort, and it was time to put the onus where it belonged. "So, how would you describe love?"

"Gravity."

"Gravity? You mean like if I jumped out of a plane I would experience the Earth's love for me in the form of gravity?" I began to laugh.

"That's right."

"So, what I felt for Dawyn was our gravitational pull?" I was getting in some good ones, now.

"It does sound ridiculous, doesn't it? But, let me ask you a question. When were the times you felt the most in love with Dawyn?"

"When we were in bed," I said flippantly and without hesitation, knowing my position on this subject was valid.

"Can you describe it?"

"You want the details?" I was just being cute but evidently we were going somewhere with this. "Okay, when we made love."

"Exactly when did you feel the most love?"

I thought at first I was going to answer "at the moment of orgasm" but as those precious memories caressed my mind I could see that the moments she and I spent just after making love were the most endearing to me. It was a time of complete openness and sharing of whatever we felt without reservation. "After we made love and before we fell off to sleep. It was like we were a part of each other," I finally said with some surprise. "Those were the times I experienced the most love between us."

"When you felt she was part of you."

"Yes, and I her."

"Then that was love, or at least the whispers of love, for love is the experience of an interactive state of oneness. It is a constant force within all hearts, and it can be felt in the physical dimension as the force of gravity. You do not generate it for it is already within you. You either allow it to radiate freely through you, or you don't."

"I don't believe it! You actually tied love to gravity. That's really clever, but I just can't buy it. I mean science has discovered other things about gravity, like strong forces and weak forces, that affect the attraction of atoms."

"What does science tell you gravity is, then?"

"Well, I have to admit I don't think they know."

"Science doesn't know what gravity is, any more than it knows what light is. . . or what consciousness is. In fact most 'scientific facts' are thrown out and replaced by new 'facts' about every ten years."

"So, I should just disregard everything science tells me?"

"The biggest disservice perpetrated by the scientific mentality is the idea that the complete truth about any aspect of life will only be acquired through the so-called scientific method of analysis. Never mind the fact that every cell in your body contains consciousness, as well as the force of love and the force of gravity. You are considered audacious or even crazy to trust your own awareness of the very things that directly connect you with the Universe."

"It just sounds too simple. People had been trying to define love for centuries; and, although there's no consensus, there is certainly agreement on it being very complex."

"This simple desire to unite is the strongest and most profound force in all the Universe. It choreographs the heavenly dance of all the galaxies; it binds the nuclei of every atom; it even creates the fusion that produces all sunlight; and it flows through every cell of your being, allowing you the experience of love within yourself, and ultimately then with another. . . . This, my friend, is love."

I took a deep breath, wanting to embrace what I was hearing but unable to totally let go of my own ideas. "If love is this obvious, how come it's so hard to see or understand?"

"Because they have inherited all of their parents' pictures and beliefs about love, everyone thinks they know what love is. But love cannot be learned through others, nor can it be experienced simply by acquiring what it is pictured to be. There is a great price that must be paid for truly knowing love."

"I'm afraid to ask."

"Most people think that the price of love is set by the person they want to love. They know they will have to comply with the other person's criteria to be loved, so they carefully evaluate what those conditions are to find out how much that love will cost them. Like when buying a car, they find the model, color, style, and accessories of love they want and then hunt for the price tag."

"You make it sound rather mercenary."

"You had a picture of what love was, and you thought you needed it. The cost of quitting your job and relocating to Colorado seemed insignificant when compared to what you expected. Unfortunately, what you thought was love was not love, and the price you paid was not what it costs to truly experience love."

"Okay, you have my attention."

"What would you pay to have a love that's greater than your heart could hold? A love that would be more exciting and more fulfilling each day, every minute of your life? A love without doubt and without end?"

"I'm still afraid to ask."

"The price for experiencing love is letting go of everything you think love is."

My attempts at love, such as they were, had been cornerstones to what I felt I knew of myself. If there was anything of which I was confident, it was that I was a powerful lover. "That can't be right. Love has probably been the most dominant factor in my life, and I've come to know quite a bit about it. I can't give that up."

"It is your beliefs about love that have dominated your life and have limited, even sabotaged, every relationship you've had."

Suddenly I felt my cornerstones slipping.

"It is only through the illogical and threatening process of releasing these preconceived notions that you can truly experience the state of oneness."

I was teetering into a mild, but familiar, depression when the telephone, for the time being, saved me. . . .

•   •   •

Just as I picked up the receiver, the thought went through my mind that it was Dawyn calling, and I was right! I would have paused to admire this exhibition of extrasensory perception were it not for the fact that I invariably had that self-indulgent thought when the phone rang. She wanted to know if One-World could borrow some fancy business phones that

I had, and she concluded with casually suggesting we get together for lunch sometime.

We met on the Northeast side of Mount Tamalpais where fewer hikers roam, especially on a weekday. As we strolled, me with a blanket over my shoulder and Dawyn carrying a small, green daypack containing water and fruit, our free hands inadvertently bumped and held on to each other in recognition of the still inexplicably strong attraction between us. We continued on, talking about everything in our lives except those things that had prevented our touching like this before now. When well off the beaten path, we spread the blanket and sat down like cautious ex-lovers. She told me of her many wonderful adventures and projects as part of One-World Family's progressive work: A trip to Russia (which we were to have gone on together) and all the travel around this country meeting with national leaders, presidents of foreign countries, and renown spiritual figures. She even had a hot tub in which to end each day, a particularly sensitive subject for me because of the hot tub I had purchased back in Denver (for her) and the fact that I didn't have one now. Her life sounded very exciting and rewarding, so naturally I was overtly happy for her.

She asked how things were going for me and, to accommodate, I engaged in an animated explanation of my book, *The Game of Mystery*, which was, aside from a little counseling and some carpentry jobs, essentially the sole focus of my life. Because this literary endeavor was not taking me to exotic places nor was it in any immediate danger of bettering social conditions, I felt it necessary to slightly embellish how far along I was with it, as well as the reactions of those who had attempted to read it. "Its premise is quite simple," I began, launching into my typical spirited description.". . . . and to either solve the mystery of 'who am I?' or win the game of 'this is who I am,' we simply use a process called 'self-balancing.' This is a process of specialized meditations from.

. . ." I'm not sure where this last bit about "self-balancing" came from. It just sounded like an interesting idea at the time, and I was hoping that my inner "friend" would later admit whispering it to me. In any event, I found myself talking on and on, adding excitement and adjectives to my sales pitch in a courageous but vain attempt to make my life sound as exciting as hers.

She said nothing, which I quickly perceived as her evaluating how I might fit into her life now; would I be an asset and would I be impressive to her colleagues? Having done a quick comparison myself, I knew I was probably losing this internal debate as she periodically glanced at the sights and sounds around us. It was just as well, for about this time I had run out of fresh material and had lapsed into redundancy.

I concluded there had been enough talking and scooted around behind her to cradle her in my arms as we both watched the setting sun. After a little while I thought I heard the voice of my inner "friend" mention something about just enjoying this silence, but an insistent question kept coming into my mind, which I couldn't resist venturing.

"Would you tell me about your relationships with Rob and Phil?"

I had known of her indulgences in at least two other relationships since the voyage of our titanic relationship; and, although fully acknowledging her right to make these mistakes, I was curious as to how she could pursue such alliances with other men when the passion I felt we had shared could never be topped. I think I wanted to hear her say that, even though I wasn't at all sure I was really as accepting of her dalliances as I was portraying.

"Sure," she immediately began without hesitation, something this question certainly called for, I thought. "I think with Rob I was being shown how quickly I can enable someone. He became very co-dependent on me."

Just like I did. I knew what she was thinking.... And, there was that word again.

"Phil was a very spiritual connection for me. He's spent several years in India studying yoga at an ashram. ...."

Okay, so he concentrated on just one discipline, but I bet my list is bigger than his.

"But, I think I completed my Karma with them and have learned what there was to learn."

Ugh, Karma again.

"If it's any consolation to you, I can tell you that my connection with Rob and Phil wasn't nearly as powerful as our connection."

There were the words, and I wanted to scream, "why did you pursue them!? Why are we like awkward cousins when together?"

She stared at my overly-controlled face. "I wish I could be different," she continued. "I wish I could be someone who wanted to have a committed relationship with one person, but I'm not."

Suddenly it was all obvious. She simply didn't understand her co-creative partnership with the Universe. In truth she could create whatever she wanted. All I had to do was help open her eyes?

•   •   •

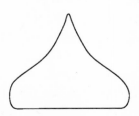

When freshly hatched power yields fledgling fright,
We flap our wings, but mostly for show,
And instead of discovering the experience of flight,
Seek only to teach others what we think we know.

Chapter Fourteen

(The **Explorer**, Warrior, Wanderer, Magician)

The Pattern of the Priest

"But, you can, Dawyn! You can have anything you want. That's the way the Universe works. It gives you the energy to live, and you can transform it into any life you want. . . ." I heard myself getting stronger with excitement and squeezed her tighter. So, this is why we had been apart—for me to learn these things about life and then be able to show Dawyn the light. Of course, now it all made sense.

"But, a relationship is just not what I'm all about. It's not what I'm here to do." Tears began to form in her eyes.

"Your life can be anything you want it to be. That's what you're here to do—choose how you want to co-create your life rather than just letting it happen to you." Boy, I had her now. How could she argue with the truth? I sat up so that we could face each other.

"My life is about giving to the world, and loving everyone, not creating a particular relationship." She looked off into the distance.

To me she was trying to save the forest while a tree in her own back yard was dying? "The next step for your personal growth lies in relationship, not out there. You don't have a fear of getting up in front of hundreds of people and sharing your heart. It's with one person in a committed relationship where your fears await."

She paused with what looked like a glimmer of recognition but still unsure. "You're wanting me to say that I'll love only you."

"No, I'm not. I never said I want you to love only me. I love the fact that you can love everyone. You're confusing the experience of love with the expression of love. . . ." I realized now that some of what I was saying was technically attributable to my internal "friend," but I figured there would be plenty of time later to explain any necessary plagiarisms required of this crucial moment. ". . . . You don't have to make love with someone just because you experience love for them." I knew that anytime now her appreciation should be kicking in for the illumination I was providing.

"Rich, that's not my intent, and sometimes those situations are results of agreements made in past lives."

The image of a candy store came to mind. "I admit we all probably have Karmic patterns to clean up," I quickly countered, "but who we choose to process that stuff with is definitely within our control. Otherwise we could never become self-empowered, we'd always be trying to follow some imagined Karmic design that has us running from one relationship to another. Actually we have Karmic ties with everyone because we are all connected at some level of consciousness." Okay, so I was totally relying now on the insights of my "friend," but desperate times call for desperate measures; and besides, I really didn't know who or what to give credit to, anyway.

"I don't believe that. For instance I think you and I have made an agreement to come here and learn about unconditional love together, and that's what we're doing."

How could she not see the truth? Maybe if she saw the incongruency of her beliefs? "We were also married on the etheric level. How do those fit in?"

"I still feel like I'm married to you. . . ."

Huh? That one caught me flat-footed and all I could do was stare in disbelief.

"I think once we make those commitments on the etheric level they are there forever and operate as such in our lives. . . . I still think of you that way."

"How do you see us manifesting these etherial marriage vows, given our current separate lives?"

"Well, I think we should see each other once in a while and express our love as best we can." She began to cry. "I wish I could be different. I wish I could be a person who could commit to a primary relationship. . . ."

Then, through my armored desire to change her, my heart gathered all my thoughts. She really did wish that, and she couldn't, and she knew that caused me pain. She was wishing she could be who I wanted and also be who she was.

"I don't want to hurt you," she said.

"I believe that and I also believe we co-create everything about our lives. You want to be free to express love in any form and with anyone you want. You'd also like to have the intimacy that only comes from a committed relationship. So both opportunities are attracted into your life, but at this point they're not compatible. This represents your own confusion about relationships."

She was pensive and sighed. "I don't know if that's true. I still don't know why things have happened between us the way they have. I just know that I have to trust the Universe, and I do still love you, Rich."

But it was a love I didn't know how to embrace. As we looked at each other in the truth of that moment, we were at once miles apart and yet never closer. Our parting was friendly but strangely subdued.

•   •   •

I spent the next several uneasy weeks doing some carpentry work to replenish my dwindling reserve of money and concentrating on merging my latest insights into my burgeoning manuscript. Then, after meditating and getting comfortable in front of my computer one night, I again approached this confusing subject with my "friend."

"So, as I was saying, what's love got to do with it?"

"I'm glad to see you still have your sense of humor."

"Barely. Well, what happened? I shared my truths and if anything she got less receptive to my insights."

"I think she did quite well. In fact she was probably less reactive than you would have been had the situation been reversed."

"That's a little bit of an exaggeration, don't you think?"

"In fact the 'truths' that you quoted to Dawyn were things that you had heard many times in your life prior to our conversations, but they made no lasting impression on you until you actually experienced them."

"Yeah, but certainly she's experienced enough in her life to be able to see the validity of these truths."

"That's not for you to decide. That is strictly between her and her Spirit. Besides, the truth others can most readily see is the truth you share through actions, not the truths you preach."

"I wasn't preaching. . . . I was passionately sharing."

"Yeah, and the Spanish Inquisition was just an oral exam."

I hate it when my opponent's retort is as accurate as it is funny. Consequently, I rarely acknowledge such cleverness.

"You have entered the next phase of the journey. Your Priest is emerging to religiously implement the newly discovered truths into your daily life. It is natural for you to also want to share these truths with others in an effort to heal their pain and confusion. However, there often develops a strong priestly aspiration to try to convert those around you in order to validate your truths and justify all your hard work. People usually try to avoid such preaching, not unlike the past readers of your manuscript."

That was a low blow, even if true.

"Any offering ceases to be a gift if the receiver has no choice of acceptance."

"Okay, even if I preached at Dawyn, surely she could see my motivation. My love for her, you'd think, would seem overpowering. How can she not be moved by that?"

"As passionate as you feel toward Dawyn, to call it love would be to hear the distant rumblings of its waves, to glimpse the setting sun dancing on its distant surface, to feel the cool drops of its early morning mist and from that say, 'I have experienced the ocean.'"

My jaw clenched, and my eyes narrowed. I couldn't believe what I was hearing. This was something I could never accept. "I was ready to die for that love."

"I believe that, but physical death is not the true measure of love."

For some reason I had always valued it that way. "Well, ready to die for her was just a figure of speech."

"If you want to measure your love, ask yourself if you are willing to face the 'death' of your identity to discover your Essence?"

I would do anything for her."

"The question is. . . are you willing to do it for yourself?"

"What do you mean?"

"The love you offer to another can never be greater than the love you offer to yourself. Wherever you block love from flowing in yourself will also block it from flowing to another."

"I love myself," I countered as if saying the obvious.

"When you and Dawyn were together the other day, you started asking her about her life-style. What was your reaction to her descriptions?"

"Well, I guess I got upset a little. She's living what sounds like a cushy life."

"And when you told her about what you were doing in your life, how did you think she reacted?"

"I got the feeling she was judging me and evaluating if what I was doing was something she could be proud of should we get together again."

"How did that make you feel?"

"Not real good."

"And when you shared your insights about the relationship, what happened?"

"Okay, I get the picture. Several things that she did pissed me off, but I think I was justified."

"Everything in your life to which you react is a mirror of some aspect of yourself."

This was definitely heading in an embarrassing direction.

"If there are aspects of Dawyn with which you got angry, it simply means that you have some beliefs which prevent you from accepting those same characteristics in yourself. These are the areas in which you do not love yourself and therefore cannot love others."

"Wait a minute. I don't have a cushy life-style."

"But there is a part of you that still desires such comforts, and you judge that desire as being wrong. And, because you do not understand that within yourself, you cannot accept it in Dawyn. This blocks you from seeing that her life-style is simply what she is choosing to co-create with the Universe in order to learn exactly what she needs to learn—just as yours is for you."

I felt like the kitchen lights had just come on to reveal both my hands in the cookie jar.

"You got angry when you thought she was judging you because you didn't want to look at those beliefs within you that judge her. It's similar to your resistance right now with what I'm saying."

"I don't feel so well," I said with a long sigh.

"That will pass."

"Thanks for the compassion!"

"There is a bright side. Once you begin to see that all blocks to experiencing love are within, you can begin to release them. Then you can truly know what it's like to swim in that ocean."

"How do I know for sure when I have a block to love?"

"Emotions."

"What do you mean, when I get emotional I have a block to loving?"

"Whenever you experience a negative emotion, it's a signal to you that you're blocking love from flowing through yourself."

"You mean I can never get angry with people again, even if someone deserves it?"

"You can get angry all you want. In fact it's a good idea to develop the habit of being spontaneous with all your emotions so that all blocks will be readily observable."

"Okay, let's say I notice that I'm angry or frustrated. . . ."

"If these emotions prevent you from remaining aware of your own Essence and the Essence of others, they are blocking love."

"Then what?"

"Anger and frustration only arise when life's circumstances don't match your pictures and expectations of how you think things should be. When you encounter such emotions, you have the opportunity to look at the beliefs those pictures are based on and decide their appropriateness.'"

"Then the anger is not the actual block to love?"

"The disruptive emotion does block love because it captures your awareness, but it cannot be released as long as the beliefs and pictures that triggered it remain."

"How many blocks to love are we talking about here?"

"Any belief can block love, especially if it generates fear or judgments."

"Let's say I buy everything you've said. . . . How would I go about finding the belief behind the disruptive emotion?"

"You ask."

"Ask who?"

"The emotion, of course."

"Wait a minute. To be rational enough to stop and ask the anger where it's coming from, I'd have to stop being angry."

"Normally, that's true, but with practice you can remain aware of your Essence, as well as the Essence of the person with whom you are upset, and also express anger. However, such an expression will be much different than when you are only aware of your anger."

I reluctantly realized my anger for Dawyn had always veiled her Essence to me. . . . "So, I just say, 'Hello emotion, where are you coming from?'"

"It's probably best to be a little more systematic."

"Like how?"

"Identify the emotion you are feeling. Let an image form if it wants in your mind. Ask this image (emotion) why it is in your life. This will reveal any beliefs and pictures you have attached to it. Be sure you understand its reasons for being there and express appreciation for its intended contribution to your life. Then, release it."

"You make it sound like going to the store and buying a quart of milk."

"Well, it can become that easy, but never that boring."

"So, seeing and releasing my blocks to love is done through this visualization process."

"Well, you actually have to focus on what you are experiencing rather than what you can visualize."

"So, it's an 'Experialization' technique."

"'Experialization!' I like that."

It was time to be totally honest with myself, especially in areas where I might have been a little lax in the past. I was prepared to face the fact that just maybe my literary work in progress was not the Pulitzer Prize material I saw it to be. Maybe my writing perspective had been influenced by the condescension of being too much of a Priest and having a blind spot or two. Maybe the non-feedback from the readers had been a message in itself. And, then again, maybe it was a masterpiece. But, at least now, after the exhilaration from this freeing Experialization, I was willing to explore all possibilities.

I would have stayed and savored this intriguing and proud moment of exploration, but I was already late for my appointment with a prospective editor. There would be plenty of time to delve further into this when my book got launched.

•   •   •

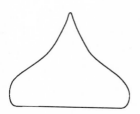

At last released from our beliefs and rules,
We see life's perfection and assume we're free,
But, such is the perspective of blissful fools,
Lulled by a little knowledge into apathy.

Chapter Fifteen

(**The Priest**, Explorer, Warrior, Wanderer, Magician)

The Flight of the Fool

We met at the Good Earth restaurant in Berkeley where she presented herself as business-like but with a relaxed air of confidence and sexuality. She was beautiful and accompanied by her adorable four-year-old son from a separated marriage. Our conversations wandered through a variety of subjects, everything except the book since there seemed to be an instant rapport between us. It was somewhere near the two-hour mark of our dialogue that I realized two things: I would much prefer this woman to be my lover than my editor; and, to greatly increase the odds of that occurring, I should probably set about rewriting my book from a less "priestly" point of view as quickly as possible.

Since she, too, was looking for the special relationship to parallel her spiritual path, the opportunity appeared heaven made, or at least certainly not by coincidence. Understandably, both of us were cautious, wanting to make sure that we avoided our numerous, respective past miscalculations in trying to attain such a partnership. So we deliberately spent the next few weeks creating a strong foundation by meditating together, sharing our respective wisdom gained from lost loves, and making sure the other could be taken out in public without creating a scene.

However, during this critical evaluation period, I could see that I had a distinct advantage. I was becoming quite adept at using the Experialization process whenever I sensed even the slightest blockage of love toward this woman, now the leading candidate for my soulmate of the year. Initially, I was shocked by the seemingly endless fears and judgments that had somehow taken up residence in my life, comprising my proud, though limited, emotional repertoire. I saw that quite possibly their subtle influences on me were the unwanted source of my appearing to be condescending and preachy at times. Moreover, witnessing the steady stream of departures as these arrogant emotional blocks were released, I realized I had probably long since passed the category of the Priest and had, at least with some friends, undoubtedly earned the title of Archbishop.

That notwithstanding, with each released block a seed of empathy and understanding seemed to take its place. Things that my new romantic partner did that previously would have irritated me became merely areas of curiosity. I saw any judgments or fearful emotions she might have as just elements of her uniqueness, and I could even appreciate their contribution to her life. Whenever something within her came up to block love, I simply sat back and watched her internal drama without over-reacting, knowing that having such blocks to go through is the way we learn about the nature of love. I didn't even expect a great outpouring of appreciation on her part for my unusual restraint in this matter; a simple "thank you" would have done nicely. But I must admit that I was just a little surprised when she mistook my enlightened behavior as being slightly arrogant and aloof (although I'm not at all sure she used the word "slightly").

Evidently, when I would take time alone to release my own blocks, she interpreted these pensive moments as signs of my not caring enough to be affected by her emotions. Detailed explanations did little to dissuade her, probably because I continued with the practice. However, I realized that her reaction of judging me as arrogant, and even claiming that I was driving her crazy, was just another of her own internal blocks to loving herself, which she would eventually see. I just kept sending her my patient understanding, that is when she could stand to be with me. My only solace was the fact that she did have a few lucid moments where she agreed with my philosophy, at least in principle, and expressed unsolicited similar aspirations for her own spiritual path. Not fully understanding her overly cautious reactions and finding myself alone one night in her front room while she read her little boy a bedtime story, I sought some guidance from my internal "friend."

"I can see how I used to act like the Priest at times, but I've moved into a whole new place of acceptance. Why is she so reluctant to join me?"

"First of all, you're not totally out of the Priest phase yet. The Spirit's Journey isn't like walking from one room to the next. You'll find that you have aspects of yourself scattered throughout all phases of the journey."

"Well, if I am heading out of the Priest phase, what's next?"

"You're becoming the Fool."

"That doesn't sound like too much of a leap for me. . . . Is the Fool a good place to be?"

"For the most part."

"Oh, this is like one of those good news and bad news routines, eh?"

"Every step of the Spirit's Journey is like that. Each phase provides extraordinary opportunities for personal growth, as well as opportunities to be seduced into staying at that step and believing you have arrived at your final destination."

"So, what's the good news?"

"The Fool is able to see that all of his actions, conscious or unconscious, are part of his co-creative dance with the Universe that will eventually let him fully experience and express his Essence. He also sees the same is true for everyone else, thus realizing that all things have purpose and that everyone is exactly on the path they should be. His goal is simply to express truth. To do so he must relinquish all need to be loved by others and yet love them enough to just let them follow their own path. The Fool's primary emotional state is that of delight, and he may often appear as irreverent and unsympathetic to others, for he enjoys life without attachment to how it unfolds. . . ."

"I must admit, I like that I'm beginning to see the world that way."

"You know, just because you can see that the Universe is perfect and there is nothing that needs to be done, doesn't mean there aren't things you need to do."

I sensed the bad news was coming. "I don't understand. If everything is perfect, what needs to be done?"

"I didn't say there were things needing to be done by you. I said there are things you need to do."

"You've lost me. What's the difference?"

"The former implies that there are things in the Universe that without your particular attention would suffer, which, of course, is not true. The latter indicates that there are things you need to do, not for the Universe, but for yourself."

Assuming I had grasped the difference, I cautiously proceeded. "Like what?"

"When at the phase of the Fool, there is a natural tendency for you to reason that because everyone is on their right path there is no real need or urgency for you to fully express your Essence or radiate love freely. Your challenge therefore is to not to be seduced by apathy."

Well, it was true I enjoyed the insights that were coming to me, but I didn't feel like they were a seduction. "So, how do you guard against being seduced?"

"Passion."

"I think I'm fairly passionate about what's happening in my life."

"Actively patting yourself on the back for seeing the perfection of the Universe is not the passion I'm talking about."

I decided to let the questionable implications of that remark pass. "You mean the kind of passion I had when with Dawyn, right?" I picked the period in my life where there could be no argument about my being passionate.

"You may need even more than that to get through the phase of the Fool and on to the next."

For some reason (like a Fool) I didn't think passion was going to be my problem, so I changed the subject to a more pressing interest. "This may sound like an obvious question, but what's the purpose of having love flow freely through me, other than it feels good?"

"Like sunshine, you don't have a choice as to whether it exists or not, it just is. Your choice is simply whether to step out of the shade and experience it radiating through. This experience of love radiating through you lets you know that you are fully expressing your Essence toward your purpose."

"So, fully experiencing love is totally up to me. I don't need to have a soulmate relationship?"

"Well, yes. . . and no. . . ."

•   •   •

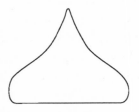

There's a reason for loving not many of us know
As we rush to realize our dreams,
But when our desire is to just let it flow,
We love others to discover ourselves, it seems.

Chapter Sixteen

(**The Fool**, Priest, Explorer, Warrior, Wanderer, Magician)

The Role of Relationship

This equivocal answer required more than a modicum of concentration on my part, which the lateness of the hour, important plans for the next day, and the sultry voice from the bedroom precluded. (Yes, we were sleeping together, but both of us were desirous of turning that common form of physical pleasure into a higher process of exploration by studying Tantra the first chance we got.)

The next morning, a Saturday, we got up early and left to undertake an arduous hike through the rolling foothills of a nearby state park. It had rained the night before, turning the designated paths to unfriendly goo, as obnoxious as any in the Amazon basin, I'm sure. Because I had failed to anticipate the obvious and chose to wear white Levi's and tennis shoes, the marsh-like terrain provided me with an immediate source of irritation. To counter the frustration from my unsuccessful and unending struggles to keep clean, I maintained a cheery attitude by trying to see the humor of my situation and translating that into a constant stream of one-liners that were, in my mind, as funny as they were entertaining. This, of course, was also a meaningful way to maintain a high level of passion as I'm sure any "Fool" would attest.

My sensual companion, however, had intended this excursion as a gift to me, since we were traversing one of her favorite places in all the world to enjoy nature. I had interpreted her resistance in displaying even polite laughter to most of my efforts as probably a result of poor hearing or not having been recently exposed to such wit, what with her separation and all. Her detached behavior simply indicated to me that she needed cheering up even more than I. So, I did what any sensitive friend would do; I refocused my attention and clever remarks entirely in her direction. After about five hours, darkness fell, relegating us to a very slow pace and leading us to believe we were lost for the last hour or so, which of course only served as added ammunition for my machine-gun humor. Seeing that nothing was evoking a positive reaction from my preoccupied companion, the thought suddenly occurred to me that her weary condition was probably due to low blood sugar, which a good meal could quickly remedy.

Our conversation was sparse during this repast, but that did not seem unusual for two tired and hungry people. Her preoccupations had disappointed me a little, but I saw no reason to add that to the growing wall between us by mentioning it. Over dessert she did manage to state that she hadn't felt especially connected to me on the hike. I replied that I had noticed her pensiveness but just assumed she wanted to stay lost in thought. We said good night with little resolution to the day; however, to make sure this potential soulmate relationship didn't go awry, I was determined to take advantage of every source of wisdom available to me, even braving a careful examination of these events with my inner "friend" while driving home alone.

"So tell me what you think is happening."

"You guys are not happy with each other right now."

"Really? If we were, do you think I'd be asking for advice?"

"A little testy, aren't we?"

Maybe I was starting off somewhat defensively, but that's only because I was invariably put on the hot seat in these conversations.

"What do you think's going on between you?"

"Well, I think she and I are just being cautious; but, yeah, I guess there's some frustration in both of us."

"Then what you've got is another typical 'soulmate,' co-dependent relationship."

"Co-dependent! Not you too. What are you talking about? We've only just begun. . . as they say."

"You actually established the pattern of your relationship when you met in the restaurant. Since then you've just been filling in the blanks."

"When we first met, we each shared how we wanted a relationship to support our spiritual paths; that's what was missing from our other relationships. . . ." My "friend's" remark was so outrageous that I began responding before my window was all the way up after paying the toll at the Bay Bridge, which quickly drew a look of surprise on the face of the previously bored toll taker. ". . . . That was the foundation for the time we've spent together."

"You'd like to think the foundation for a relationship is established through the words you both share, but it's not. The basis for any relationship comes from your basic perception of life."

"But we both see our approaches to life as spiritual, not co-dependent."

"Calling a cow a horse doesn't mean the saddle will fit."

My head cocked in confusion, but I don't think I would have responded to that mixed metaphor even if I had known what it meant.

"Two people meet, each with extensive criteria as to what their respective ideal relationships need to be like. Whether these expectations are called spiritual, romantic, financial, or whatever, they all share the commonality of generating pictures as to what each needs from the other to be happy; and as long as the two people look to the relationship to fulfill needs, that relationship is automatically co-dependent."

Recalling my surreptitious and semi-extensive research on the subject during my break up with Dawyn, I hesitated to quote the "experts," knowing that tactic to be rarely successful in past conversations with my "friend;" but finally I succumbed to the temptation. "That's not what I've read about co-dependency."

"Do these authors on co-dependency agree among themselves on what it is?"

I didn't think they did, but I wasn't going to admit that at this point in the discussion. "I think they suggest that co-dependents are people who subjugate all their own desires and lose themselves to their partner."

"The co-dependent is someone whose self-definitions and beliefs are considered negative and whose attempts to control life are covert. A so-called healthy person is someone whose self-definitions and beliefs are considered positive and who overtly seeks to control life. However, the co-dependent and the healthy person both cling equally to their respective identities, and they both seek to control relationships in order to have their needs met."

"So, I'm being co-dependent in this current relationship even though I want it to be spiritual?"

"If you have some expectations and beliefs about how it should work, it means you are approaching the relationship through your identity-based reality, which automatically produces co-dependency."

I shook my head wondering if I'd ever get this relationship thing right.

"The signals to let you know are your own frustrations, even if only slight, toward the other person. If you had no needs or expectations for her to fulfill, there would be no frustrations, and no blocks to loving her regardless of what she does."

"Well, then you're saying that even healthy relationships are co-dependent?"

"Sure they are. When you meet a prospective soulmate, isn't it nice if she says she needs you?"

"Yeah, I like to hear that I'm needed."

"That's because it feels good to do things for others, and it also puts you in a good bargaining position. You know that if she's dependent on you to fulfill her needs she's much more likely to be motivated to meet your needs."

I shrugged from this uncomfortable truth by reaching to turn on the windshield wipers as a light rain began to fall.

"Trying to avoid co-dependency in identity-based relationships is like trying not to get wet when swimming."

"So what should people do, start seeing a counselor on the first date?"

"Hey, that's cute. But, when you are counseling couples as a family therapist, what is your basic process?"

I had to concentrate. . . . "Basically for each to identify what they want from the relationship, communicate those things clearly, and realize that it is a give-and-take process that requires compromising on occasion."

"Since you both have different needs that you want the other to fulfill, the goal is to become civilized and friendly adversaries, right? And, compromising adversaries eventually come to accept that not all of their needs will be met, so they settle for, even become content with, a relationship that is less than what they really want."

"I'm getting depressed."

"Or, they cling to their respective pictures of happiness and become bitter enemies, eventually leaving that relationship only to repeat the same scenario with a series of prospective soulmates."

"I am depressed."

"For you, the idea of compromising what you pictured you needed as a soulmate seemed like a betrayal of your dreams, consequently you would continually go on to that next potential special person rather than negotiate with the one you were with."

"No need to get personal," I said with a heavy sigh as the rain became intense.

"But, there is another role for relationships, one that provides for a true soulmate bonding."

"It's about time." I took a deep breath. "I thought this doom and gloom was going to go on forever."

"You asked last night if you needed a soulmate-type relationship to fully experience love, and I answered 'yes and no.' No—you can fully experience love flowing through you without ever co-creating a soulmate relationship. Yes—such a special relationship provides an unequalled arena in which all of your own blocks to love will come up for you to see and release, that is if the relationship is based on your Essence instead of your identity."

"Well, that's what I want to do in this current relationship, and I think that's what she wants, too."

"An Essence-based relationship is one in which neither partner harbors the expectation that the other has to fulfill even one need. . . . Both make only one commitment—a commitment solely to themselves to participate fully in the relationship with the specific intent of removing all their own blocks to love so as to experience a true state of interactive oneness."

"Well, come on now. A relationship has to meet a few basic needs. I have a need for affection from the relationship, and I want an agreement of monogamy, and I also want intimate communication, to name but a few."

"Instead of looking at these desires you've mentioned as needs, let's say you simply decide that you are the kind of person who wants to live your life being affectionate, being monogamous, and being a communicator of intimacy. So you make a commitment to yourself to live your life in this manner because you have found that in living this way you are able to more fully express your Essence. Consequently, there is nothing your special person has to do or be for you to experience the desired fulfillment of your commitments. You have taken total responsibility for yourself."

"But, what if my partner stops being monogamous or stops being affectionate with me?"

"You see? That's an identity-based fear. It's based on the belief that, unless you get your partner to commit to you, you won't have any control over getting your needs met. That's why in a typical relationship both people spend their time trying to find out what each other's needs are, negotiating mutual commitments around those needs, then trying to make sure such promises are kept."

"But, when I made commitments to Dawyn, I made them out of my own free will. I truly wanted to do things for her, whether she asked me to or not."

"Did you ever make commitments to her without the desire, indeed the expectation, that she reciprocate with some comparable commitments to you?"

This was getting hard to look at. "Well, that may be true, but we never asked each other for specific commitments."

"Needs and expectations are mostly unspoken, yet conveyed in very subtle and persistent ways."

At that point, even though I continued to argue, I knew my "friend" was right. I just didn't want to think of my relationship with Dawyn as identity-based, and I certainly didn't want to admit it was co-dependent. "I have the feeling that if I approach someone saying, 'I'll take care of my needs and you take care of your needs' the relationship will be artificial in a way, and there won't be that 'magic' of falling in love."

"Yes, the 'magic' does feel different in an Essence-based relationship, for it is not dependent on ever changing physical attributes, nor confined to the limits of mental pictures, nor does it fluctuate with the whims of temporal emotion. Instead,

198 / KARMA Covered Candy

the love that flows between you both will be based on self-love, unfettered by fears, judgments, and desires. Both of you are free to share yourselves, not from the adversarial position of negotiating needs, but from the open-hearted posture of true friends who seek only to enjoy the full experience and expression of Essence as you share your respective journeys."

"Well, you're describing the ideal relationship where, if and when she didn't keep her commitments to herself, I would just point it out to her and all would be well again. But, that just wouldn't happen. There's always problems and friction."

"You're right."

"I am?"

"An Essence-based relationship can be an emotional roller-coaster."

"It could? Worse than my relationship with Dawyn?" Even though I was playing "devil's advocate," I was hoping there would be answers for my objections.

"I wouldn't say worse, but at least ten times greater than that with Dawyn's."

"My heart couldn't take it," I said, partly as a joke, but as I heard the words I realized I believed them.

"Actually, your heart yearns for nothing else."

"How do you know?" I asked with curiosity, not defiance.

"Of all the things you could be doing in your life you stay focused on this quest for truth, and the feeling that you do have a special love waiting for you is always present."

I sighed. It was true. "Tell me why an Essence-based relationship would be such a traumatic process. . . just on the off chance I ever have one!"

"The more love that flows through you both, the more each of you feels the overwhelming desire to experience a total state of interactive oneness with each other. Anything and everything within you that prevents that unity, every fear, every judgment, every dark shelf will be illuminated to be embraced and released. Many of these things will be so painful to look at that you will blame your partner, get angry with her, and even want the relationship to end rather than deal with the fear and confusion of your identity."

"Then how can it survive? If it's going to be ten times worse, I mean greater, than Dawyn's, how will we hang in there?"

"You'll stay because you will have experienced each other's Essence and know on that level that you are connected. Also, you will have the courage to go through these fears because it is a commitment you have made to yourselves, not to each other. No one ever goes through the horrendous process of self-discovery just to please another. . . . For your Spirit's Journey, to whom have you made this commitment?"

I didn't know exactly how to answer that. I remembered when I consciously stated my intention for this journey a while back and it got a laugh, but I also knew I had been struggling with this all my life. I simply could not be doing anything different. . . . And, now I had the information to co-create an Essence-based relationship. All I had to do was call up my current potential partner, explain to her the reasons why we had run into our recent problems, and begin again on the basis of not fulfilling each other's needs. For the first time in a long time I felt in the eminent proximity of a real soulmate relationship.

•   •   •

"Let me get this straight," she said in a slightly less pleased inflection than I had anticipated. "You want our relationship to proceed on the basis that you are not going to fulfill any of my needs and I don't have to fulfill any of yours?"

Repeated back to me from her less than enamored perspective, the concept appeared to have lost something in the translation. "Well, there's a little more to it than that. . . ."

"Look, it's hard for me to concentrate on this right now. I've been processing what went on between us the last time we were together and, if you're open to it, I'd like to talk about the hike."

I knew this couldn't take too long. After all, that was just friction between our identities, and we would soon be abandoning that archaic process of relating. "Sure."

"I've thought about it quite a bit, and I feel the teasing comments you made that day were kind of a put down to me. They were said to try to get a laugh, but they all seemed to come from a dominating position or attitude. . . ."

I began impatiently chewing on my lower lip. "Humor is one of my most sincere and intimate ways of communicating," I thought to myself, finally concluding, "She doesn't even recognize love."

"I even felt that some of your cavalier comments were somewhat derisive, as if letting me know that you were superior. . . ."

My fingers tightened their grip on the phone, and my jaw clenched. "Where was this coming from," I wondered. "Was she that insecure? Well, she may not be ready for a soulmate relationship, after all. Not only does she not have a sense of humor herself, she misinterprets the humor of those around her." I remained within myself until she became more direct.

"Do you have a response?"

"Well, I feel myself becoming very defensive, so there must be some truth to what you say." Where the hell did that come from! "I trust your intuition, so it's something that I'll look at." As I heard the words come out of my mouth, I realized that indeed I was consumed with defensiveness, and looking at myself through her eyes was the last thing I wanted to do. So, why was I saying I'd do it?

"Can I tell you something more?" There was extreme caution in her voice.

"Of course," I said without any obvious hesitation.

"I don't think what you did was directed toward me personally. I think it's your way of responding to women. . . . I think it represents an animosity you have as a man toward women in general. . . ."

A shutter slithered through my body with that thought. I immediately heard a chorus of voices in my head proclaiming that I love women, that I'm fascinated by women, that I respect women, that this idea was absurd. Yet, I could say nothing aloud in defense. . . .

"Did you hear me?"

I began nodding my head before realizing she couldn't see that response. "Yes," I said a little above a whisper.

"Do you have a reaction?" she asked in a higher than normal voice that slightly cracked with the last word.

"Only that I feel an overwhelming desire not to look at this."

Our conversation ended cordially with her repeating that she didn't think she wanted to let go of her needs being fulfilled in a relationship. Alone in silence again, I took a deep breath and rubbed my forehead and temples in slow, deliberate circles. I could feel my defensiveness turning to embarrassment, though I didn't really know why. I played back in my mind the jokes and anecdotes I had offered on that hike. They still seemed humorous and innocuous in their intent. I shook my head while exhaling audibly.

"What were you feeling toward her that day?"

The comforting though unexpected appearance of that familiar voice brought a half smile to my face and a quick shrug. "Nothing unusual. We had just made love, so I was feeling a little cocky, I guess. I always experience a little extra pride on such mornings after. But, other than that, everything was normal."

"And, what is your 'normal' feeling around a woman?"

"I'm usually a little excited because of the natural attraction. I usually become more active since being around a woman brings out my maleness."

"Anything else?"

As soon as I heard the question I did see something else, but it wasn't real clear. "I guess I also experience a little fear. . . probably because I want the woman to like me so I'm a little on edge, a little cautious to make sure I don't screw up."

"Why don't you do an Experialization on that right now?"

"You mean just go back and experience what I felt on the hike?"

"Sure."

That didn't seem like an unreasonable request, especially since I had said I would. I shut my eyes and within a few minutes of using that process I was reliving the day in question and remembering some of my witticisms with renewed clarity causing me to snicker in mild appreciation.

"See if you can get in touch with that part of you which you describe as 'a little on edge' when around women."

Suddenly, the whole picture changed. I could still see myself walking along making jokes, but within me, just behind my smiling grin, loomed an austere face of intense vigilance, as of an ancient sentry dressed in ominous dark armor. Throughout the entire hike, he never took his eyes off my companion, alertly watching her every move with an unblinking suspicion. I nervously wondered what this presence was. . . and why I had never seen it before.

•   •   •

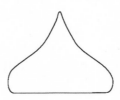

We each spend our lives on a personal quest,
*   A cherished desire amid all fortunes faced,*
But every dream is sought in jest,
*   Until our Self we've finally embraced.*

Chapter Seventeen

(**The Fool**, Priest, Explorer, Warrior, Wanderer, Magician)

The Reunion of Wholeness

"What is this sentry figure you sense?"

I had no idea. To answer that question I had to go back in my mind to the hike and look at it through the eyes of this dark, inner figure. As I did, my heart began to pound and my face grimaced with resistance. "He fears her, and he. . . he hates her!" I didn't want to believe it. I would have argued forever that nothing even remotely like hate was in me.

"Ask him why?"

The figure didn't answer when I queried. Instead, still through its eyes, I began to see scene after scene, as if floating through centuries of time, and in each of the scenes there were various smiling, joyful women of all ages and appearances. I felt the familiar seductive attraction toward each, but slowly my desire for these women was overshadowed by a growing fear of them; and their smiles turned to looks of caution and defiance. Then, right behind my fear came a consuming imperative to control them, and again their faces changed, this time to reflect anguish. I had the sense that there was even violence occurring in the scenes passing before me, but only the terror on the faces of these unknown, familiar women was painfully clear in my vision. My stomach tightened. "Why are you here with me?" I silently screamed at the dark figure.

Again it did not speak, but somehow I knew he was a protector, a guardian. He saw women as the source of pleasure and happiness. But he knew he could not attain such gifts if the woman withheld them. Woman was therefore his greatest desire and also his greatest fear. The only alternative to this threatening dilemma was to use his superior strength to control and dominate her, and then by sharing his joy with woman, she would find her fulfillment.

"Not in me," I said over and over in remorse. I knew intellectually that women had been mistreated and abused by men throughout time but had excused it as something of the past. Maybe some men were still sexist, but certainly not any in my circle of friends.

As I continued to watch through the eyes of this apparition, I witnessed again the day of the hike and this time could see that many of my comments had been filtered through this fearful perspective. Many contained the veiled but determined desire to control the woman I was with, and it was all done with a smile. The more I looked, the more I realized that my ignorance of this sentry's negative influence was not confined to just that sojourn in the woods; it had existed throughout my life. I was ashamed. . . . "Have you known about this. . . whatever this is within me?" I asked of my "friend" in a tired voice.

"Yes."

"But, you didn't mention it because I wouldn't have believed you until I experienced it for myself, right?"

"It's nice to know that our time together is not being wasted."

"This isn't funny," I retorted impatiently. "Is this figure supposed to represent something I've created in my past lives?"

"I didn't think you believed in past lives?"

"Until now, if this is."

"This sentry is your heritage, the legacy of love between man and woman throughout time. It is part of your Karmic bond with the history and with the nature of mankind."

"You mean I've inherited this guy?"

"Precisely."

"So this sentry is like an instinct I have toward women?"

"That's one way to look at it. During their lifetimes the attitudes of your father toward women and those of your mother toward men were seeded in their respective genes. When you were conceived, their genetic tissue united to create some basic perspectives that are now contained in every cell of your body."

"This dark figure in me is something I inherited from my mom and dad?"

"Not just your parents. Each generation inherits the tendencies of all previous eras and then adds their own beliefs and attitudes to that inheritance. Your instinctual posture toward the opposite sex, which is what the sentry represents, is the accumulated experiences of relationships from your particular lineage throughout history."

"Wait a minute. You're saying this influence is actually contained in my cells. To change it or release it, what do I have to do, have radiation therapy?"

There was a laugh before its reply. "That would probably make it worse."

"Well, that's helpful. So I'm just stuck with this curse?'"

"Consider it your cellular Karma."

"So what's the antidote for cellular Karma?"

"Nothing."

"This is not what I want to hear. There's got to be something I can do to purge this guy. Isn't there some sort of genetic laxative I can take?"

"If there were, you'd be in the bathroom a long time."

I wanted to laugh but the implications were too disturbing.

"When I say 'nothing,' I mean nothing more than you're already doing. As you express your Essence more and more in your life, love naturally radiates through your body erasing these inherited influences."

"But I'm not even completely sure what my Essence is. How can I know when I'm really expressing it and not just something I think it is?"

"There are five basic qualities of action that, when consciously embraced, ensure that Essence is being fully expressed. The first is honesty. . . ."

Believing this was going to be more than a one sentence answer, I reflexively reached for my note pad.

"More than just telling the truth, this means being trustworthy, not allowing anyone to believe what you, yourself, don't believe. . . . Next is integrity, having the courage of your convictions even when it may cost you something. . . . The third is fairness, offering the same consideration you wish in return. . . . Then there is the simple gesture of showing care and respect for others. . . . And the last is being spontaneous with your emotions and actions."

There was a pause as if waiting for my scribbling to catch up.

"When you consciously employ these five qualities in what you do, your Essence will automatically be expressed, and you will experience love radiating through you."

I took a deep breath feeling now that I could begin to diminish this sentry's current influence, yet I still felt badly about the past. "But, even if this dark presence fades, how do I make up for the way I've treated the women in my life?"

"That you see this sentry is the only important thing for now."

"Come on, I've got to do something. This is like finding out that my father is really Darth Vader!"

"Okay. There is one thing you can do—you can go dancing"

"Again!? Is that your answer to every dilemma? . . . sort of the metaphysical equivalent of take two aspirin and call me in the morning? I've already gone dancing, remember? I was thinking of something more redemptive, maybe something along the lines of writing every woman I've known a letter that explains my recent discoveries and. . . ."

"And what?"

"I don't know. Ask them to forgive me. . . . Oh, I forgot, there's no such thing as forgiveness. . . . Well, at least explain why. . . ."

"If a special event is what you want to occur, then it will, but my advice to you is to take my advice."

I laughed at what I thought to be a joke, probably designed to take my mind off this recent discovery whose unresolved aspects were quickly inducing sleep. . . .

•   •   •

Fortunately, I was able to set the whole quandary aside for a day to keep a previous commitment to Sabina (my E.T. friend) by attending a luncheon for some entrepreneurs wanting to put more "Spirit" into business. She was going to perform (sing) and wanted a supportive face in the crowd, something I not only knew I was qualified to do but also felt would be a pleasant hiatus from my current preoccupation. Everything occurred as I would have anticipated at this gathering, until I felt a strange attraction to one of the speakers at this function, a diminutive woman in her forties, with shining eyes and an undeniable presence. My attraction to her was not sexual, just a strong curiosity; although given my testosterone level, I'm sure it wouldn't have taken very much to ease it in that direction. I inexplicably sought her out and signed up for one of her classes on body awareness and movement. Of course in hindsight I realize I should have known it was going to be a "dance" class, but at the time I didn't make the connection with my "friend's" advice. I thought I was doing this one all on my own.

The best description of this class would be modern or interpretive dance, probably the one activity I had been most diligent in avoiding all through my life. And it was just like I had dreaded it would be—surrounded and out-numbered by independent women in their own element. I was the only man in the group of eight, dressed in my far-from-flattering dull blue running shorts amidst the fluorescent flurry of mostly bulging, but some very shapely women in brightly colored leotards, leg warmers, and head scarfs. Although trying my best to be inconspicuous, with all the mirrors in the studio I couldn't look in any direction without being face to face with at least one of them. Once I was able to overcome my initial awkwardness, self-consciousness, hostility, and overall terror, I actually began to enjoy the activity, but by then the class was ending.

It must have been in this weakened "after glow" condition that I signed up for the entire series of classes that met twice a week for the next few months. I even decided to blend in by acquiring some colorful spandex garments of my own. The funny thing was that in my leotards (which I must admit looked pretty darn good on me) and leaping around barefoot in front of mirrored walls with several unconcerned, similarly dressed women, I experienced a freedom I had never known, or even knew existed. Every time I looked at my reflection during this artful hour and a half, which was quite often actually, I smiled with surprise and growing confidence.

Surviving these sessions and even feeling better because of them apparently weakened my embarrassment threshold. On the proverbial bulletin board at this dance studio was a flyer proclaiming the virtues of Rolfing, a deep-muscle massage technique designed to release emotions that are stored as tension in the body and highly recommended by most of the ensemble as a way to further enhance the body-mind-Spirit connection. Overriding the expected wave of anxiety and for no logical reason, I followed another bizarre inclination to sign up, even though it was definitely an activity I had previously considered effeminate.

The perpetrator of this enticement turned out to be an innocent looking middle-aged woman whose hands, any two fingers of which could easily compress a beer can, should have been registered as lethal weapons. This was not "deep-muscle" massage; it was "beyond-muscle" massage. I never knew bones could bend. But, as promised, the process did release feelings, namely the constant desire to defend myself. Tears did come to my eyes a couple of times, however that's also happened to me on occasion at the dentist's office (such oral excavations I now consider to be pleasant ways to spend an afternoon). At the merciful conclusion, I felt secure in the knowledge that every painful cell in my body was working perfectly; yet I couldn't help wondering if these cleverly disguised Nazi war criminals would ever be brought to justice.

After hearing of my brush with death, my fellow dancers convinced me to try a more gentle school of massage, one that didn't have the dubious distinction of giving out black belts to its practitioners. I did and was able to humanely experience my body's collection of stored emotions.

Engaging in these previously considered feminine activities precipitated an unusual increase in my sensitivity. An avid movie buff, I found myself crying at the slightest dramatic provocation and, even more surprisingly, enjoying it. I also found myself interacting with waiters, waitresses, salespeople, and the like with uncommon spontaneity just for the fun of it. And strangest of all, I realized I had begun to express how I felt about things rather than what I thought about them.

However, I still wanted some significant and distinct occurrence to mark the release of my unwanted cellular Karma and to at least partially atone for my questionable treatment of women in the past. I hopefully assumed I would

210 / KARMA Covered Candy

get some indication of what to do on my now annual summer climb of Mount Shasta, five days away. My two previous adventures with the mountain had provided spectacular experiences; but just for insurance, I planned this year's ascent to coincide with a full lunar eclipse. Besides, it had now been almost a year since outwardly choosing this Spirit's Journey, which meant, if my "friend" was reasonably accurate, that I was nearing its end, a milestone that would undoubtedly be marked with at least as much panache as past, less significant moments in my life. Little did I know. . . .

•   •   •

For the next three nights, I had the same disturbing dream. In it, I was standing in line at my bank, a new facility that had plexiglass sheets across the counters protecting the employees from would-be robbers. As I approached one of the available, encased tellers, a gunman appeared, grabbing me from behind, holding a gun to my head, and demanding that the bank give him money or he'd do me grave harm. Somehow, I got into a violent and lengthy struggle with this shadowy, menacing figure. I became so angry I wanted to kill him. Each morning I awoke in a sweat from this nightmare but tried to dismiss it as just a dream. On the afternoon of the fourth day, while reluctantly looking in my bathroom mirrors and debating whether to shave the insistent stubble on my jaw, I happened to notice an ugly, irregular dark patch of skin hiding behind my right ear. Its size, about that of an odd shaped quarter, suggested its unobserved presence for quite some time. Concerned, I touched it and, though it felt no different than the surrounding skin, I tensed, instantly realizing that this was the exact spot where the malevolent adversary in my dream had pressed his gun against my head.

My doctor, a bright engaging woman of about thirty, looked at it the next morning. "It's a melanoma," she stated without hesitation. "The only question is how far it has progressed into the layers of your skin. That we can't know until it's removed, which we're going to do today, and then have it biopsied, which takes about a week." She went on to explain to me, as reassuringly as she could, the insidious nature of this cancer; but my mind drifted away. All I heard were the words my "friend" had said to me about twelve months earlier when I had asked about the length of my Spirit's Journey, "Given your current condition, you have about a year left."

•   •   •

Dazed from the ominous turn of events in my life, but not wanting to mope around the house waiting for the lab report, I proceeded to my planned reunion with Mount Shasta. Following my usual route up the mountain to the top, I was, as expected, exhausted. I had wanted to stay at the summit but it was much too cold to consider, even for what promised to be a dazzling view of the impending eclipse. I was headed back down by late afternoon, a little disappointed about the uneventfulness of the hike so far, but looking forward to the evening's cosmic drama. I camped at about the ten-thousand-foot level on the southern slope and was not disappointed. The moon rose over the slightly hazy horizon as a brilliant lavender ball already in full eclipse. Being in the Earth's shadow, the moon's roundness was much more apparent, giving it a depth and texture not usually perceived. For the next hour or so it slowly rose in the sky, gently reassuming its customary glow and gracing the mountain and the surrounding forests with a surreal day-time appearance. I decided to hike out rather than try to sleep in this eerie light.

The next day, still desiring some kind of personal omen from the Universe, I headed on foot for an enchanted spot called Heart Lake, which I had heard was somewhere in a national forest area west of Shasta. Several hours later after traversing a few, thickly wooded ridges, I surprised myself by stumbling onto a meadow that, hidden behind a grove of pines and nestled up against a granite cliff, cradled a small green lake shaped roughly like a heart. Because of the steep surrounding hills, the sun seemed to go down early so I quickly made camp. I continued to be depressed because of my medical uncertainty, and also because I still felt strongly that I should be doing something to make up for my previous attitudes toward women. Since nothing seemed to be going as hoped, I just wanted my mind to go blank. Finally, a little sheepishly, I checked in with my "friend."

"You don't really need a special sign from the Universe. There's an easy way to atone for your actions. . . ."

I wasn't sure how to respond, for I had the impression from earlier conversations that there was nothing I could do.

". . . . And, you've already done it!"

I could hear the glee in its tone for having surprised me again.

"By consciously choosing to do things in your life that previously your male dominating beliefs prevented you from doing, you have begun to honor yourself and to experience life from a more balanced and whole perspective."

I wasn't sure of the connection. "How does that make up for what I may have done in past relationships?"

"To achieve the experience of wholeness within yourself is to give meaning to every relationship you've had. . . . This is why Dawyn came into your life."

Hearing that, I immediately wondered why I had never before asked about that.

"You both were looking for something from the other in order to feel whole, but that's something that just can't be acquired through another."

I smiled with the familiar sense of her presence, which never seemed to be far away from me.

"You've wanted every woman you've ever known to make you feel whole. It's no wonder you attracted Dawyn into your life."

I stopped feeling so sad. "So, you're saying that her Karmic agreement was to show me how I was treating women?"

"Dawyn enabled you to experience the quality of your love."

"But, after Cindy I wanted to change the way I loved. Dawyn and I were going to create something much different, that was our Karmic agreement" I nervously picked up a few small pebbles and began skipping them across the glassy surface, causing disruptive ripples to invade all corners of the lake.

"You had no idea of how deep your old pattern of loving went until Dawyn."

"Come on. . . I treated her like a queen."

"Trying to get her to fit the image of the woman you wanted. . . . What's the worst thing you've ever done. . . in your whole life?"

I scooped up some more small rocks while reluctantly searching my memory; I really didn't want to concentrate on the worst things in my life. . . . It seemed every relationship I'd ever had contained some ugly moments, but I really couldn't say which was the worst. "I don't know,"

"The thing you are most ashamed of."

I suddenly relaxed my arm, which was just about to hurl another projectile into the excited water. There was no hesitation as one incident stood alone. About two years before I met Dawyn right after the failure of my third marriage, I was living in Sunnyvale with Natasha, a three year old Rottweiler (dog) I had raised from a puppy.

"But, surely this isn't what you mean? This had nothing to do with relationships," I protested aloud to the silence of the forest, while my thoughts continued unabated.

I had trained Tasha, as I affectionately called her, extensively on my own and took her with me just about everywhere I went. She was, by her own nature and breeding, completely devoted to and protective of me. I considered her my most prized possession and loved to show her off. When she came into heat around that time, and knowing Rottweiler puppies could be sold for up to a thousand dollars each, I decided to breed her, carefully secluding her in the backyard until I could locate a suitable pedigreed mate. To my horror, I returned home from work one day to find some "mutt," actually a neighbor's shepherd mix who frequently played with Tasha, had broken through the fence. Although both dogs were just sitting innocently on the grass, they were panting heavily with open, tongue-draped mouths, and had obviously just finished smoking a cigarette. Seeing the expected ten thousand dollars slipping away, I was livid, but merely kicked the "rapist" out of the yard and called the Vet. I would just get her an abortion and wait until her next heat to shop for a new car. Unfortunately, every Vet I talked to told me any abortive procedure would likely render Tasha sterile. The only alternative was to go through with her pregnancy, that is if she were.

She began to show about half way through the eight-week gestation period. I got so pissed off every time I thought about it that I told no one of the situation and relegated Tasha to the garage, only taking her for walks at night. I just wanted the whole thing to be over with, and the next month could not go by fast enough. Finally, coming home very early one morning from a most forgettable date, I discovered that Tasha was not in her prison, evidently having pushed her way through the nailed-shut dog-door to get into the backyard. I grabbed a flashlight and followed the unmistakable, squeaky sounds to the far corner of the yard where, under a bush, sometime during the night, Tasha had curled up and given birth to eleven multi-colored puppies. She looked up at me in the artificial light with a strange mixture of fear and exhausted pride as her wiggling, noisy brood nursed from her belly. On many occasions during the two previous months I had thought about the options of this moment; but when it came, I only saw the course of action that would bring the least amount of embarrassment and hassle for me. While Tasha carefully watched and sniffed, I gently lifted each puppy and placed it in a box, which I then quickly carried back to the garage. Tasha immediately jumped up and followed as far as the side door where I barred her entry. I sat the box down on the workbench and covered it with burlap. . . . Within a short time all the puppies. . . .

I began to writhe, letting the pebbles I had been tightly squeezing fall pathetically to the ground so that I could hold my head. I did not want to relive this.

"And the puppies died."

"Yes," I lamented with a shallow sob, forced to return in thought again to that night.

I went to bed thinking that I would just get up later that morning and everything would be like it was before. But Tasha got no sleep. She continued to run from door to door, anxiously trying to catch a glimpse of me or her stolen treasure. Finally, I went out and tried to get her to play or do some tricks, but she would have none of it, continuing only to sniff and search for her puppies. It was too hard on me, so I left her alone. Finally, after about fifteen hours of this, she suddenly stopped, as if responding to some distant command, and crawled through an open ventilation duct in the foundation to get under the house. Nothing I could do would coax her out, and here she would remain for the next three days and nights.

During this time I vacillated between extreme guilt and tremendous anger. Finally, in desperation, I cut an opening, large enough to squeeze through myself. On my stomach, I slowly snaked my way along the moldy ground through the dark, cob-webbed clearance beneath the floor joists until I was within a few feet of her. I had figured that I could talk her out or, if need be, pull her out. As I shined the small flashlight in her direction, our eyes met, and I knew she "knew." She was not angry. Her heart held nothing but sadness and pain, and I could see that because of what I had done she was deciding whether to live or die.

"That moment was the worst moment of my life," I whispered through my salty lips and began to rock back and forth as my stomach tightened with a painful shame, reducing my breath to a series of noisy spasms. . . but the memory continued.

Unable to speak, I awkwardly backed out of the narrow crawlspace. Not knowing what else to do, I simply remained sitting in the backyard feeling totally helpless and, in anguish, trying desperately to understand why I had done such a thing. I couldn't bear the fact that she was in so much pain nor the thought of losing her, much less the realization that I had selfishly caused it. I even prayed, but felt so very far away from God. . . . About three hours later I felt something very familiar touch my hand, and I quickly opened my eyes. Lying next to me, just as she had done so many times before on our joyful forays into nature, was Natasha, her weary head tilted to one side and resting again against my leg. . . .

"It was this callous action, as much as any past relationship, that brought Dawyn into your life."

I was having a hard time thinking and it seemed my entire body ached. "What do you mean?" I asked while lifting my head to sniffle and take a deep breath.

"Tasha trusted you with the most precious thing in the world to her, in fact her very reason for living, but being so dominated by your male perspective, you did not see its value to her and you let it perish, leaving her with the pain and sadness of not knowing whether to live or die. Dawyn came into your life so that you could experience the separation within yourself caused by such male dominance. . . . With Dawyn you gave birth to what you believed was a brand new love, greater and more precious than any you had previously known. It was a love that enabled you to feel whole and gave you a reason for living. You trusted her, but in your mind she let that love perish, leaving you faced with the decision whether to live or die. In this way you were able to experience the way your unbalanced love manifests to others. It all happened perfectly."

I shook my head in disgust.

"Such actions occur for everyone when they establish a separation within themselves that prevents the experience of wholeness."

My thoughts of gratitude went swiftly back to Tasha and the many happy times we had together after that day. "You know, I just can't release the memory of those puppies," I said feeling my emotions beginning to well up again.

"That memory is Tasha's gift to you without condition, reminding you always to love yourself as much as she did, and then give that love to others."

I wondered if I could do that.

"Tasha and Dawyn are equal players in your Karmic game of mystery."

I smiled at the reference to my dormant manuscript. "What do you mean?"

"The pain you feel you gave to one and the pain you feel you received from the other were necessary for you to reach this point of experiencing yourself. If there are such things as prearranged agreements that are made and kept to facilitate spiritual growth, then your relationships with these two are as Karmic as they get."

I must have fallen asleep after that because at some point in the night I awoke to a familiar melody, and in a semi-lucid state began to see off in the distance of my mind's eye a purple sphere, appearing similar to the eclipsed lavender moon the night before. As it slowly floated closer, I realized that it was the start of a familiar dream, the one in which I'd often see the image of the woman meant for me. In this approaching sphere, as usual, was the beautiful dancing woman with long dark hair. Only this time, the violet bubble was coming close enough for me to make out the features of her face. As her expressions changed, I seemed to experience the associated emotions. If she looked sad, I could actually feel her sadness, and with her smile I felt elated.

Suddenly, she was right up against me, the purple sphere with its inner rainbow hues surrounding us both. As a beautiful radiance, she leaned toward me, and we enjoyed a tentative embrace. Unbelievably, I could actually feel her warmth on my neck and her hair caress my ear. I took a deep breath, inhaling her special fragrance. Still in a peculiar slumber, I felt my body moving rhythmically in the noisy nylon sleeping bag as we swayed in unison. What a marvelous dream this is I thought and wondered if it meant I was finally going to find my life partner. At that precise moment she whispered:

"I love you."

My body tensed. "Oh, my God," I said, catching my breath and urgently sitting upright. Positioning my back against the tree to my right, I pulled my knees up to my chest and cradled my head with my arms in a rocking motion. The waning moon had long since completed its arc across the clear sky leaving only the distant stars to light the small mountain glade, whose soft, gentle breeze now carried the sounds of my muffled sobs through its misty shadows. Tears rolled down my face, some of joy, some of shame. The words just spoken to me were from my internal 'friend," and I now knew who this "friend" was—I knew the truth. . . .

•   •   •

From distant drums and on roads less travelled,
We begin to seize that awesome power imparted,
Finding at last the mystery of life unraveled,
With the courage to take the journey uncharted.

Chapter Eighteen

(**Fool**, Priest, Explorer, Warrior, Wanderer, Magician)

The Portal of Destiny

My emotional catharsis continued until the morning light. . .
. The indigenous finches and sparrows with their musical,
flighty chatter at last invited me to open my eyes. Nocturnal
ground mice, retreating to their burrows, had left small uniform footprints as decorations on the dusty earth all around
me. Through the trees, the top of Mount Shasta was visible
many miles away, with the morning sun about to make its
appearance just to its right. At last I could speak.

"You wanted me to just call you 'friend,' but you are more
than that to me, aren't you?" She didn't answer, and I didn't
expect her to for I could now distinctly feel her presence. She
was smiling. "You are the feminine part of me, the part of me
that I have denied all my life. . . . It is you I have been searching
for in every relationship, hoping to become whole again. . . .
You are that soulmate of my dreams, aren't you?" I lowered
my head again, unable to contain my emotion.

"There is nothing more to learn from sadness and everything to learn from joy."

"How could I have been so blind?" I rubbed my forehead
roughly, trying to ignore her typical kindness.

"It is the nature of the identity to separate the male and
female aspects of the Self. But, in truth, you and I have never
been apart."

I scooted down to the water's edge letting my feet sub-
merge into the soggy layers of unidentifiable ooze on the cold

lake bottom, closing my eyes to again see the violet vision of my feminine side still floating all around me. I lost all ambition other than enjoying this complete moment with my "Self." . . . . It may have been hours later when I returned to thinking.

"What shall I call you?" I asked, almost as an afterthought.

"I am known as Sarra."

•   •   •

Instantly another wave of emotion washed over me, overflowing my heart. My thoughts raced over the implications of her being the Sarra of the parables in my dreams, but it was beyond my comprehension. I could do nothing but look aimlessly with blurry eyes at the rippling water and slowly shake my head. I thought of all her stories over the last year from which I had gathered so much, and then realized she'd actually been with me a lot longer than that. "Thank you for your wisdom," I muttered, wanting to express so much more.

"I have said nothing to you that you did not already know, otherwise you would not have recognized it as truth. Besides, in a very real sense we have merely been talking to our Self."

"You are my intuition, aren't you?"

"Well, you know what they say, it's a dirty job but someone has to do it."

Off guard from the prior solemnity, I burst out laughing amid some lingering tears and began coughing uncontrollably. . . .

"A major component of everyone's intuition is that aspect of themselves from which they have separated. That's why intuition always knows the external path that will lead to internal unity."

"Then everyone is on a quest to find a soulmate in a way?"

"Regardless of the desired object or stated objective in

life, each person is trying to reclaim wholeness, because it is only then that one can truly experience and share love."

The sun was fully visible now, with rays sifting through the lower branches of the weathered pines to lift a silent mist from the lake before abruptly ending the long journey by bouncing up against the watermarked granite cliffs that rimmed the west bank. I could feel the timelessness of life as I pulled my feet from the cloudy water and began thumping them vigorously on the ground.

"So, what's next?"

"The question is never 'what's next?' The question is always 'what's now?'"

"No, I meant what's next in our life."

"I know what you meant. You're eager now to know our destiny. So, let's go."

I took this to mean break camp, which I did in short order while managing to maintain my euphoria. Unfortunately, being in ecstasy does not lend itself to accepted navigation procedures and, within a short time, I found myself in very unfamiliar terrain. I noticed also that the forest shadows were quickly growing in length as twilight approached. However, my extraordinary emotional state did afford me one distinct benefit in this situation—I didn't care. I simply continued walking. . . .

"Congratulations. We have arrived."

Sarra's words brought my attention back to a mental place of conversing. I obviously had been skipping along the darken trail in this unattached state for quite some time. Glancing around and still seeing nothing that looked familiar, I wasn't sure what she was referring to; so I figured I'd rest awhile at a clump of rocks about twenty feet further along the incline I was traversing. Upon reaching that higher spot, I found myself at the top of a high cliff looking down on the familiar sight of my truck in a deserted parking lot about two-hundred feet below. I started to be amazed but then just smiled.

"Well, not quite. I still have to make it down these rocks," I cajoled, while leisurely glancing around to spot the easiest way down and wondering if the forest critters had found their way into the camper where I had more trail mix stored.

"No. . . . It's the Spirit's Journey I'm referring to. We've arrived at the portal to the last phase."

·   ·   ·

I had heard the word "portal" only once before that I could readily remember. It was the title of a Star Trek episode in which Kirk and his comrades encounter a strange circular contraption meant to be a multi-dimensional doorway of sorts called the Atomichron. The time on the other side of this large arching trellis could be adjusted into the past or future so that one walking through would emerge into another era, another reality.

"You mean we're at a doorway?" I asked rather tentatively, sitting down to rest and noticing the snow crowned Mount Shasta in the star-lit hazy distance.

"Exactly."

There was an unusual excitement in her voice, and I suddenly felt a strange premonition. Just as Sarra had known we were back at the parking lot, she must also know what the biopsy was going to show. "You mean the portal of death," I said as if accusing. "You know how the lab tests are going to turn out, don't you?"

There was no immediate response to my accusations. I was prepared to be really annoyed if this were to be the far from glorious end to my quest, not to mention my life. I had not yet accomplished anything meaningful nor did I have even a prospect for sharing true love, both of which had been part of her advertised inducements for undertaking this journey.

". . . . The cancer has served its purpose."

"What?"

"Bodies are funny that way. They self-destruct when being used for things other than the purpose for which they are intended. Fortunately, ours got your attention before that occurred."

It sounded like Sarra was saying the biopsy would be good news, yet I wasn't at all sure I completely believed this concept about bodies being able to communicate. "You're saying our body created that melanoma to tell me something?"

"Our body is an equal partner with us on this journey. It will communicate with us one way or another, even by using cancer."

"So, the cancer was just a message, and if I hadn't got the message. . . ."

"Even with this cancer, and even with all your past notions of suicide, death is not the portal to which I am referring."

Her tone seemed condescending, as if I'd never been serious in my previous plans for self-destruction. "And you're going to tell me I was never really going to do it?"

"Your pain served to show the depth and character of our Spirit, neither of which would ever succumb to those passing, shadowy thoughts."

That completely undercut my initial defiance, and I felt my emotions rushing again unchecked. In a way, I was actually relieved to acknowledge that I couldn't have gone through with it.

"No, death is unimportant now. The portal I refer to is our portal of destiny."

I had come to trust Sarra a great deal since first hearing her voice, so I wanted to match her upbeat tone but couldn't. I looked down toward my truck below and the life to which I would be returning. My journey had brought me to the edge of a cliff in more ways than one. This was not destiny, at least not the destiny I had gone through this arduous life for. Perplexed, somehow I did not feel like I had arrived anywhere in particular. Even though Sarra seemed unconcerned, the possibility of cancer still clung to my mind. I was scared.

"There is one more thing we need in order to go through this portal and claim our destiny."

"So, what is this final step?" I asked trying not to display my caution.

"Vision."

"It's not my eyesight I'm worried about right now," I said with a cynical shrug.

"Cute, but I mean it's time to create a vision for our life."

"Don't you think it might be more prudent to wait until we get back and find out the results of the tests before making any long-range plans? I couldn't resist injecting a more than slight parental tone since logic was finally on my side.

"Oh, I guess I was mistaken. I thought I heard you say that what you wanted from the Universe, more than anything else, was to experience your destiny and to know true love."

Nailed again. I couldn't even enjoy some totally justifiable self-pity. "Not to change the subject, but can I ask you a question? Sometimes you refer to us as 'you and I' and sometimes you refer to us as 'we.'"

"Yeah, when you do something right it's 'we,' and when you screw up it's 'you and I.'"

I had to laugh realizing that was the kind of answer I would have given had the situation been reversed.

"Actually, I'm still used to talking to you as if we were separate, just as you do. But, it's coming back to us. . . . So, do we want to go through our portal?"

I relented. "Okay. Let's see, what would be a good vision for my. . . I mean our life?" My nearly, but never, completed book came to mind, but it didn't seem altruistic enough to be acceptable. Contributing some way to such causes as the homeless or abused children popped up, but they didn't seem personal enough.

"I'll give you a clue. . . happiness."

Oh, I saw where she was going. "You mean if I can think of the project that will give us the most happiness, we can go through this portal?"

"Well, actually it works a little differently than that. To go through our portal of destiny, we have to leave happiness on this side."

"Wait a minute. Why would we want to do that?"

"To live consciously in the moment, we must release all pictures and beliefs of what happiness is. In so doing we are free to envision all possible opportunities for fully expressing Essence and radiating love, the natural joy and happiness of which cannot be comprehended by the identity."

I sat back with a deep breath and curled my lip. "So, to achieve my destiny, I have to let go of everything I know that makes me happy?"

"Don't worry. We'll still go to movies, and eat ice cream, and even make love. . . ."

I was somewhat relieved, but I knew better than to relax too soon.

". . . . but not as an escape or diversion from the routine and unrewarding aspects of life. The true experience of happiness is naturally attained only while being conscious in the moment, regardless of what we happen to be doing.

Although her words made beautiful sense, I was still unsure. "But, even if I did let go of what I believe happiness is, we're nowhere near accomplishing anything we're here to do."

"And, what is it that you believe we are here to do?"

I hesitated, wishing I had given this some thought prior to opening my mouth. "Well, I don't have an exact vision. . . but, I know we're here to do something very important. . . ." I only needed half my brain to throw out these platitudes while my other half raced to come up with something meaningful. ". . . . I have the feeling sometimes that our destiny will be making a lot of money and creating a philanthropic foundation that can contribute to some significant changes, like ending hunger or finding a cure for cancer."

"Which would be a more important vision to have, assisting in a research project to find the cure for cancer or driving a school bus?"

The answer was too apparent, especially because of my current medical uncertainty, so I concluded that this must be, in another twisted type of reasoning, a trick question. However, I decided to go with my first inclination anyway, confident that my present circumstances would lend themselves to its defense. "The cancer researcher."

"It would seem so. But, what if this researcher was so dedicated to his vision that he neglected his family, becoming alienated from his spouse and kids and ignoring all relationships with others just to immerse himself in this noble quest. And the bus driver, on the other hand, developed loving relationships with his family and friends, and lived his simple vision by sharing this love with all the school children who rode with him. What then?"

"Still, the cancer researcher might develop a cure that could save thousands of lives. It would seem that the sacrifice of a personal life is worth the greater vision," I concluded with confidence.

"What has been the greatest contributor to death and suffering in mankind's history?"

This sudden change in the topic generated that familiar sinking feeling in the bottom of my stomach. "I don't know. . . . I guess war."

"War is caused by perceptions of being separate and the resulting feelings of indifference, the inherent result of maintaining an identity. As long as we experience a separation within ourselves, we will be separate from others. As such, we can justify and rationalize everything we do, even killing one another. Having a noble vision like cancer research while adhering to one's own identity-based illusions serves ultimately to perpetuate the entire system of indifference and separation, and does not help awaken others to their Essences and to love."

I reluctantly thought of people from whom I felt separate and toward whom I felt indifferent. . . .

"Better to use the moment consciously, even if merely driving a bus, than to spend that same moment unconsciously, though seeking the cure to cancer. . . . So, which vision is the most important?"

"Okay, in the situation your describe, the bus driver's," I conceded.

"Actually, no vision is more important than any other."

When was I going to learn?

"All visions do the same thing—provide opportunities to express our Essence toward purpose. But no vision is, in and of itself, our destiny, even if that vision leads to finding a cure for cancer."

I did not readily welcome this thought. I had always pictured myself at some point standing back from an important accomplishment and saying, "I have done what I came here to do. I have achieved my destiny." Such an achievement would have to begin of course with a noble vision.

"So it doesn't matter what vision we have?" I challenged. "I can just pick any vision and go through the portal?"

"We may have dozens of visions in our life, heading toward one for a while and then seeing something else that is more appropriate to do. That's what visions are for—to be like lighthouses that guide the expression of our Essence in certain directions during different phases of our journey."

"Without a definite vision of our destiny, how will we know when we have truly achieved it?"

There was a chuckle. "Our destiny is not to be found in the promises of any vision."

"I don't know if I understand."

"Imagine that you've just achieved the greatest ambition you've ever had. . . . and you're standing there, basking in that accomplishment. . . ."

No exact picture came to mind. I just knew I wanted to have my life in some way be an acknowledged positive influence.

"It doesn't matter what it is, or even if you see it clearly. . . . Just imagine that you have done it. . . ."

"Okay."

"Now really get into it."

I immediately pictured a fantasy like winning the Nobel Prize. . . .

"How do you feel about yourself in relationship to the Universe?"

"I feel ecstatic. . . . I feel complete. . . . I feel like my life has been justified. . . . And I feel on top of the world, in total harmony with the Universe."

"And how did you feel as you walked through the woods today?"

Realizing that how I felt this afternoon after embracing Sarra was the same as I had imagined I would feel at some point in the future when achieving my destiny, I couldn't answer; and another wave of ecstasy washed over me.

"Destiny is not the destination—destiny is the journey."

·   ·   ·

These words gripped me like none before.

"Our destiny is not what we will do, but what we are doing—not what we will become, but the ever unfolding experience of who we are right now."

So much was coming at me so fast, and now I was being asked to give up even my vague but important impressions of destiny, something I had previously clung to at all costs.

"Everyone wants to see themselves as the apple picked by the noble King rather than the one salvaged by the common serf. But, in truth, the apple's destiny is simply to be as pure and sweet as it can be so that the Universe can use it as it will. An apple doesn't ask itself what it is here to do because it is too busy doing what it is here to do."

I turned my head and thoughts toward the shimmering sky. "So, my sitting here right now. . . is my destiny?"

"Our destiny."

"Sorry, our destiny. And whatever the results from the lab report will equally be our destiny?"

"Bingo. . . . No moment in our life is any more important than any other moment"

This can't be! "So, let's see if I've got this. To go through this portal of destiny, all we have to do is let go of everything we think happiness is and pick a vision that will help us stay totally conscious in the moment. . . and to fully express Essence. . . and radiate love?" Although beginning the sentence somewhat facetiously, I slowed down as I finished, actually listening and being affected by my own words. "And what happens, exactly, when we go through this portal?"

"We enter the final phase of the Spirit's Journey, that of the Artist."

A melody awaits within the heart,
Released only by one's own hand,
Contributing from each an essential part,
To this magnificent symphony called man.

Chapter Nineteen

The Music of the Artist

"So, we're no longer the Fool?" I asked while shifting my weight to a more comfortable spot on the rock.

"Attached to that title, are we?"

I laughed, realizing that I was.

"We'll always be the Fool. The Artist not only sees the perfection in everything, just as the Fool does, but also the beauty and the interconnectedness."

"So how does the Artist differ from the Fool?"

"Well, for one thing, the Artist enjoys always expanding his passion for life."

I knew I was being kidded a bit for thinking that I had enough passion already. "And how does the Artist apply this passion?"

"The Artist is the Fool who consciously uses the Universal Laws and Principles every moment so that all thoughts, emotions, and actions are expressions of Essence and integral to his life's purpose. He has completely awakened from the dream and relates to all others through Essence rather than identity. The Artist lives each moment as if it were brand new and sees everything in life as if for the first time. Since he no longer experiences any aspect of his being as separate, his faith and trust in the Universe is absolute. His primary emotional states are passion and serenity; and his one ambition, regardless of his lot in life, is simply to fully express Essence while radiating love."

The idea of my being able to live that way was exciting. "Why is it called 'the Artist?'"

"Because in this phase of the Spirit's Journey, we are musicians, expressing our Essence as if it were a rare melody. Our life is the instrument for that music, and love is the conductor that weaves together the diverse melodies of all people to form the symphony of man. . . ."

I was feeling a tremendous pride in these thoughts and the fact that they were coming from my own feminine nature.

"Did I also mention that in going through this portal we will find that relationship we've always wanted.."

I jerked forward. From the tenor of the previous revelation, I had assumed there would be a long hiatus in the conversation while I digested its relevance. "My soulmate relationship, finally?" I said while looking up and laughing out loud, noticing that I could actually say the word "soulmate" without my heart becoming arhythmic.

"Yes, as the Artist, we can finally recognize that special relationship."

"Recognize?! I thought you said soulmate relationships are chosen," I blurted out a little confused.

"They are."

Unbelievably, I found myself getting even more excited. "So, which is it? Will our soulmate be someone we choose or someone we recognize?"

"Yes."

"Why do I feel like I'm Lou Costello asking who's on first?"

"Our soulmate is someone we choose, because she is someone we recognize."

"Well, then how will we recognize her?"

"We really don't have to be concerned about recognizing her. . . ."

"Why?"

". . . . as much as making sure she can recognize us."

I sheepishly realized this particular minor aspect had been slightly overlooked in my excitement.

"Only an Artist will recognize another Artist."

"By consciously expressing our Essence and radiating love, right?"

"Right. . . . At least, all this is what I think is going to happen when we go through the portal."

"What do you mean 'you think?'" I was used to always hearing certainty in her voice.

"Hey, I told you I haven't gone all the way to the end. We can only go through our portal of destiny and become the Artist together."

"So, we would be equal partners from here on out." That thought scared me, but it also brought a degree of satisfaction. However, I was still stuck on one other thing. "If we don't really know what's going to happen, what's the motivation for us to take this last step?"

"There is none, at least not in the usual sense."

"Then why would we do it?"

"Because, that is who we are."

I paused.

"I could give you some altruistic reasons; but, in truth, for those who see this Spirit's Journey, there is no choice. Therefore, reasons have no meaning. We stop seeking happiness elsewhere because that allows us to experience our natural state of happiness. We are passionate about life because it allows us to experience the evolution of consciousness unfolding in our daily actions, and to be a full co-creator with the

Universe. We care, because we know it is through us that the Universe can care."

I stood up and paused as a powerful shiver ran down my back. In that instant I slowly but inexorably realized that it also didn't matter what the biopsy showed. Either way I could, if I chose, live each moment as my destiny. . . . I began to cry; it was the only expression that felt completely appropriate. . . . Finally, with tremendous gratitude, I whispered to Sarra, "I love you." But, as the words floated into the night, I realized I was, at last, saying them to my Self.

•   •   •

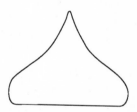

Epilogue

She hesitated, surprised at first by my calling and then with the impromptu invitation to go to the ocean. It was overcast but warm enough to walk barefoot along the shore to where the dunes meet the surf at the north end of Stinson Beach. There we sat and talked.

I wasn't exactly sure why I asked her; I didn't have anything prepared to say. I simply knew I had to see her. I guess I wanted to tell her what I had gone through lately and what I had learned, and maybe that I wouldn't be treating her badly anymore. But, as I began, there were no words to convey what I felt.

We stared at each other in silence, as we had done some many times before long ago, but now our hearts were merging through moist but wiser eyes. We kissed. Her lips were unexpectedly warm. I held her in my arms for the first time— for the first time without fear.

It was because of Dawyn, more than anyone else, that I had found my Self, and the portal of my destiny. I made her my greatest love because I believed she had what I needed to be me. And then I made her my greatest fear because she had the power to take that feeling away. If she were not the person she is and had done anything different, I would still be in the consuming struggle of trying to find happiness outside myself.

I was feeling immense gratitude for that, but that wasn't why I was now holding her tightly in my arms. I also knew that I was in her life to reveal her lessons as much as she had mine. And we would do that for each other just by being ourselves.

No, as I squeezed her I understood that I was with her now for absolutely no reason, other than a pure expression of love. Like in the beginning, I again felt the divine experience of my heart overflowing, yet totally at peace; but this time there was no shadow of fear. I didn't want her to change or make any promises, nor did I even care whether she loved me or not. And, because there were no conditions, I could not tell where my love for her stopped and the love for myself began.

I had addictively spent my whole life searching for the very stuff that naturally wanted to flow from my heart all along. For some reason I had always pictured a truly loving another as being different different than this, which is why it always was. Now, there was just love. . . and if I could feel this way with the one from whom I had felt most betrayed and for whom I had felt the most fear, then I was free.

We smiled together, for the gift of each other, somehow in our silence having known there would be this moment of completeness. . . and beginning.

•   •   •

Appendix

The Guiding Universal Laws and Principles*

I. The Law of Consciousness

- The Principle of Self
- The Principle of Mutual-Choice
- The Principle of Identity
- The Principle of Essence
- The Principle of Intuition
- The Principle of Purpose
- The Principle of Resonance

II. The Law of Co-Creation

- The Principle of Default
- The Principle of Power
- The Principle of Attraction
- The Principle of Abundance
- The Principle of Reflection
- The Principle of Sovereignty

---

* Refer to <u>TOTAL EMPOWERMENT</u> for complete description. (See notice in back of book.)

III. The Law of Love

- The Principle of Conditionality
- The Principle of Wholeness
- The Principle of Relationship
- The Principle of Happiness

IV. The Law of Change

- The Principle of Cycles
- The Principle of Connection

Available later this year:

TOTAL EMPOWERMENT

The Complete Guide to Success, Love, and Happiness

by
Richard Treadgold

Author of KARMA Covered Candy

Contains state-of-the-art technniques for co-creating every-thing you desire, as well as a complete list and description of the **Guiding Universal Laws and Principles.**

Would you. . . .

- like a greater level of success in your life?
- like more love in your life?
- like happiness as your daily companion?

Are you. . . .

- ready to learn how to co-create everything you desire?
- ready to learn what love really is and how truly loving relationships are formed?
- ready to release the those things that block your natural state of being passionately happy?

If so, then GET **S.E.T.**

Self-Empowerment Training

Not a therapy!
This is a state-of-the-art training for:
- those interested in understanding and consciously utilizing the Guiding Universal Laws and Principles to co-create life.
- those wishing to remove the blocks to achieving a greater level of success.
- those ready to incorporate techniques that allow for complete mastery of emotional states.
- those desiring to experience unconditional love.
- those wanting to discover and express their Essence.

─── **Certificate** ───

$25.00 Value

Submit this certificate when signing up for *S.E.T.* and receive a twenty-five dollar discount.

─── **Certificate** ───

Order and Information Form

Name: _____

Address: _____

City: _____

State: _____ Zip: _____

☐ Yes, please send me information about getting *S.E.T.*

☐ Yes, I like a copy of TOTAL EMPOWERMENT at
the pre-publication price of $9.95 ($10.95 retail).

Item	No.	Price	Total
Total Empowerment		9.95	
KARMA Covered Candy		9.95	
Tax (Calif. residents add $ .70 per book)			
Shipping ($2.00 / First book: $1.00 each additional)			
		Total	

Send check of money order to:

     Essence Foundation
     P.O. Box 16418   Section C-3
     San Francisco, CA 94116

Please allow two to three weeks for delivery.

Index